— THE SUITCASE —

JAN DANIELS

First published by Busybird Publishing 2020

Copyright © 2020 Jan Daniels

ISBN 978-1-925949-79-7

This work is copyright. Apart from any use permitted under the *Copyright Act 1968*, no part of this publication may be reproduced, stored in a retrieval system or transmitted in any form or by any means, electronic, mechanical, photocopying, recording or otherwise, without the prior written permission of Jan Daniels.

Cover design: Busybird Publishing

Layout and typesetting: Busybird Publishing

Busybird Publishing
2/118 Para Road
Montmorency, Victoria
Australia 3094
www.busybird.com.au
Phone: 03 9434-6365
Email: blaise@busybird.com.au

CONTENTS

Chapter 1:	THE LEAVING – PART 1	3
Chapter 2:	PAULA	13
Chapter 3:	THE LEAVING – PART 2	23
Chapter 4:	COMING HOME – PART 1	35
Chapter 5:	THE GAME – PART 1	39
Chapter 6:	IN THE BEGINNING	45
Chapter 7:	COMFORTABLY NUMB	55
Chapter 8:	CONTROL, ISOLATION, SHAME, LOATHING	59
Chapter 9:	HOW TO KILL A HUSBAND	71
Chapter 10:	THE BEGINNING OF THE PLAN	73
Chapter 11:	A STRANGE KIND OF LUCK	81
Chapter 12:	COMING HOME – PART 2	89
Chapter 13:	THE GAME – PART 2	93
Chapter 14:	GAME CHANGERS	99
Chapter 15:	RUN FAT NANNY, RUN	103
Chapter 16:	SETTLING IN – A NEW LIFE	111
Chapter 17:	THURSDAY NIGHT	115
Chapter 18:	UNDER THE KITCHEN SINK	117
Chapter 19:	KILL ME NOW	123
Chapter 20:	THE SLUT OF RAMSAY STREET	129
Chapter 21:	WELCOME TO THE KOALA HOTEL	133
Chapter 22:	LOSING IT ALL	137
Chapter 23:	MY LOVE AFFAIR WITH MADNESS	143
Chapter 24:	THE LEAVING – PART 3	147
Chapter 25:	HOW TO BUILD A LIFE	153
Chapter 26:	LET IT BE 2015	157
EPILOGUE		161
ACKNOWLEDGEMENTS		163
ABOUT THE AUTHOR		165

For my children, it was always for you.

To Jasmine, Matthew and Devon who lived the reality, together we built a fortress – it has never been broken. We always win.

And for Paula, who was brave enough to be my friend.

PREFACE

This book has been a long time in the making.

Many a time I had put it aside, not wanting to share my vulnerability with the world. However, despite the trauma and pain in revisiting this time in my life, I also wanted to celebrate the things that matter, the things that kept me going towards a dream of freedom and a better life.

I also hoped in some small way to shine a light on the isolation and challenges of living within a violent relationship, and the judgement of a society that simplifies the situation with the suggestion to 'just leave'.

From the depths of isolation, fear, and madness, to the highs of sunshine, song and freedom, this is my story. From breakdown to breakthrough, and the realisation that no suitcase is needed for the things we truly value in life.

In the January of 2003 I packed a suitcase.

I was again homeless, only now there was just me.

I had packed away everything I had left of value in my life and stored it in a friend's garage.

I moved in with my mother. I had left that house 29 years and three days earlier.
It was the day I married.

I had made a long journey home.

My suitcase and I.

1

THE LEAVING

PART 1

There were no bruises in sight. He wasn't that silly, yet my muscles and bones ached, and my ribs were pained with each inward breath. My head still throbbed where he'd dragged me around by the hair, pulling me across the cold of the lino, the grit of an unswept floor digging into my skin.

It must be now. I have to get away.

I have to survive.

'Mummy, Mummy, Mummy,' broke the stillness of the day.

As I stood on the verandah, an uneasy agitation began to crawl within my body. Sweat trickled from my skin in the constricting heat. I felt its burn rising from the concrete in shimmering waves of colour; with each inward breath, the north wind seared my nostrils. The children ran through the sprinklers, arms flailing as they attempted to catch the water, hair plastered against their necks as the water trickled down their faces, their tiny feet dancing as they dodged bindies on the parched grass.

'Mummy, Mummy, Mummy.'

Momentarily mesmerised by the sparkling colours of water and sun, I watched on in silence as the rapid water jets hit their tiny naked bodies. The children waved and smiled up at me whilst continuing to play, laughing and shrieking with delight, unaffected by life and the stifling heat. A smile made its way into my heart, and my face softened with a remembered pleasure of childhood without the burden of fear looming large, casting a shadow as it hovers above me. I appreciated the stillness of the moment, so simple and carefree. *Would it ever be that way again?*

The sounds of children rang out through the quiet of my home, which stood on top of a hill in Anglesea, the road leading up to it a no-through road. There were only five houses in the street and we lived in the second last house at the end, surrounded by nothing but the beauty of natural bushland. As far as the eye could see, there was the majestic beauty of the magnificent gumtrees and Australian natives. To my right were my beloved clifftops and just in front of them were the tea trees, the only plants that seemed to survive the harsh sea breeze. These overgrown tea trees served as a great playground for the kids to make cubbies and play hide and seek. Twisting through the tea trees was a back track to the beach below the cliffs. For the children it was a secret world, a bush playground. Nestled close to the clifftops of Anglesea, surrounded by bushland, there was no one to hear them but me. With the urgency of a photojournalist with a rapid-fire camera, my memory saved these pictures of a time that was. Little did they know we were hours away from our final escape.

It had seemed years in the planning. Several thwarted attempts later, I carried the scars of my attempts to leave. This time I had planned it carefully, no clues, no emotion. *It must be now.*

The pain and humiliation of the night before played through my mind. Redness flooded my face – even with no one here to bear witness, I still felt the embarrassment and shame.

I had been ordered by him to go out into the darkness of the night, to walk the mile and a half to the local pub to get him more beer. Petrified of the dark and embarrassed to walk into a men's bar, I had steadfastly refused and held my ground until eventually I had been beaten into submission. I set out down the gravel road, past the bushland trees that seemed to whisper and hide frightening forces. Every now and then I would stop to listen for any footsteps following me on the crunchy gravel, as the deafening thump of my racing heart bruised my chest from within and furtive eyes tried to make out shapes and shadows in the dark. Clinging to the comfort of my big woolen cardigan, I wrapped it tight around my broken body and distractedly patted my hair with my hands, wiping the dried tears and fear off my face on the cardigan sleeve. I just hoped there were no visible marks on my face, as the embarrassment would be too much to bare. I should have checked the mirror that sat on the newly painted wall near the front door. I still would have had to go into the night – vanity is a luxury; it made no difference what I looked like.

As I half ran down the darkened road to the rhythm of my beating heart, the headlights of a car approached up the hill. I slithered into the bushes to hide like a hunted animal, shrinking into the surrounds as I held my breath, fear echoing in my ears. Up ahead I saw the lights of the pub. My heart sunk, knowing that all the local drunks would be gathered in varying degrees of sobriety around the bar. I would have to walk past them to get to where they served alcohol. No doubt they had heard all the stories of the nutcase woman who lived on the hill; well now it seemed they were all about to meet her.

Squaring my shoulders as I pushed open the heavy bar door, I felt the silence as they stopped drinking long enough to take in this disheveled mess standing before them. Avoiding their eyes upon me, I headed straight to the counter to order the box of beer. I had not really considered the weight or my ability to carry the box home as I made my way past the drunks. Feigning a strength I did not have, I managed a polite thank you as one gentlemanly drunk held the heavy door open for me. I felt his eyes of pity upon me.

Once outside in the cool night air, I tried to adjust the weight as I began the hill climb home. Walking in the darkness, cloaked in shame and fear, I knew this was the moment. I would leave everything behind and make my final escape.

From out of my quiet reflections, remembering the humiliation and pain of the night before, I am jolted to the here and now as I hear a car travel up the road. The slow crunch of gravel and cloud of red dust in its wake signals that he is home. With a casual wave of my hand I muster the calm smile of a perfect doting wife. I need everything to look like it's OK.

Slamming the car door, he saunters past me into the house and heads to the fridge. He must quench his thirst in this heat, and a cold beer is his drink of choice. The fact it is mid-morning means nothing as he finds the daily newspapers and sits in his chair.

I really need to find that old suitcase – where did I put it? Trying to think of the basic necessities, I go through a mental shopping list in my scattered brain as I ponder what I should pack, where I could be going, and what I need.

I am hauled back from my musings by the sound of the children squealing and laughing in the mid-day sun. They seem to have forgotten it is lunchtime and I am grateful they are occupied, as it would give me time to plan and pack. As their laughter brings me back to this moment, I see him watching me, head cocked to one side as he looks at me quizzically.

Does he know what I am thinking or suspect what I'm going to do?

A thousand horses seemed to be racing in my chest as I felt the heat of colour flood into my cheeks. I swallowed hard as the heaviness sits in my throat like liquid chocolate, threatening to make me vomit.

'Focus Jan, focus,' I told myself. *'Get it together.'*

He grips the side of his faded club chair – the pattern long gone, worn away with beer stains, the smell of cigarette smoke ingrained in the material. With the pressure of his arms and body he'd embedded his comfort and being into its structure. He rises with purpose, the springs of his anger taut. I hold his piercing blue gaze as he walks over and kisses me lovingly on the cheek, as if nothing had happened the night before. His hand gently caressed my face, the bony knuckles sending a remembered pain through my body. I took a slow breath to keep calm – no trouble, no suspicion. He looks into my eyes, looking for clues, looking for answers. I remain still and small – the child within playing hide and seek, wanting desperately not to be found. Gripping my chin, he directs my face to his, forcing eye contact. I continue to hold my breath until finally he turns away and makes his way to the garden to follow the sound of the children laughing and playing, seemingly satisfied in my subservience. As he walks past our eldest daughter Jasmine he gently ruffles her hair then, grabbing the hose, he aims it at the younger children. Matthew grabs onto his little sister Devon's hand, her toddler steps not fast enough to escape getting soaked. The children run away laughing, their squeals ringing loud in the peace of the bush. With relief I let out the choking breath that had been burning in my lungs, and casually follow him outside.

I watch from the verandah as he makes the children laugh with silly jokes. He tickles their tummies and continues to splash them with the hose. He chats to them about their day – what have they been doing, have they been anywhere, who have they seen, has anyone visited Mummy? Always looking for clues. It all seems so normal – the happy family enjoying the sunshine, the loving father gently kissing his daughter's head before he makes his way back to the house.

I nervously follow a few steps behind, the sycophant servant following her master. I am trying desperately to keep everything normal, not wanting to arouse suspicion or give him any reason to stay home. No need to rock the boat, not now, not today. I watch carefully as he surveys the room, a puzzled look on his face. Inside I freeze. Heading to the fridge, he grabs another beer and returns to his chair, the king to his throne, the ruler of all he surveys.

His focus returns to me. With increasing dread, I feel the red beam of his laser eyes piercing me. *He will kill me if he suspects I am planning to take his children away, that I would dare to live a life without him.*

Placing an unsteady hand on my stomach to slow my panicked breathing, willing my body not to betray my emotions, I fear I am emitting signals like a lighthouse beacon. Distracting myself from my paranoid thoughts, I begin wiping a benchtop with more vigor than necessary. Knowing how to give him cause for something to say about nothing, I casually suggest a chicken salad for dinner.

'Well don't fuck it up,' is his sullen reply. 'In fact, I think I'll finish early today. It's too fucking hot to work.'

Naturally I agree that this is a good idea and nod as he rants about work, the dickheads he works with, the wages, the government and a long list of other things that have annoyed him today. At least he's not ranting about me and my long list of shortcomings – so I automatically switch off, pleased that I have shifted his attention to everything else that is wrong in his world.

After finishing his cold beer, he finally gets up from his chair in a swift jolting movement. 'I'll be home about 12,' he bellows over his shoulder as he makes his way down the hall to the front door.

The carefully displayed ornaments sitting on the hallway table rattle and shake, and the mirror on the wall shudders on its fragile hook as the door slams shut. *Quiet relief.* Thankfully it seems he is returning to work after all, so I silently thank whatever god is above.

***

Finally the time came. Slowing my breathing to calm my nerves, the sickening anxiety was building up within my body from what I was about to do. A huge knot in my stomach seemed to be coiled so tight, like a snake ready to strike. Walking with a newfound purpose to the front verandah in my attempt to gently gather the children, I then recoil and retreat. He's still there, kneeled on his haunches and talking quietly to the kids. They stand there dripping wet, listening to him, still and earnest.

'*Just go,*' I whisper, '*just go.*'

Suddenly he turns to look at me and seems to scan the house. *Does he know? Is it a trick or a trap?* I wonder? I obligingly wave him goodbye, the weight of my arm feels like someone else's.

The sound of gravel crunching, and that familiar cloud of red dust, signals his departure.

For a moment I stand there frozen. *This is it* – ninety minutes exactly.

I snap into action, fear and adrenaline kicking in. The old suitcase is hopefully still hidden in the shed. Now faded and tattered, it is covered in spider webs. I brush them away with an urgent hand; now is not the time to worry about spiders. Hurrying towards the children's bedrooms I grab a few things I think we will need – shorts, t-shirts … what else do I need? Only one suitcase, what shall I take?

Out of the corner of my eye I see the three ceramic mugs my mum had bought the children as an Easter gift, their names painted on one each in thick black paint. *Jasmine, Matthew, Devon.* Yes, I must take those. Come to think of it, Mum bought me a ceramic ornamental china man – yes, I must take that, too. What about me, what do I need? A nightie, I'll need a nightie … although I sleep naked. I can't do that where I'm going.

I start to throw things that catch my eye into the suitcase. Time is running out. I remember to take some identification, I am quite pleased with myself that I had thought of that. I had learnt the importance of this over the years from past efforts to escape.

Now where did I hide the money? Where had I put it? I search frantically in cupboards and drawers, panic making me not see for looking. I finally find a folded twenty dollar note hidden in the back of a kitchen drawer, thank goodness. It had always been so difficult to hide away a stash of money. I was not allowed to have any money of my own just in case I did decide to make a run for it, or make a phone call for help. Being financially dependent kept me there, trapped. During the times he sent me out to buy beer, I had begun to sneak the left-over change when he was too drunk to know what was going on. This was indeed my small victory. I took a small a moment to enjoy it as I tucked the twenty dollar note into my purse.

I hurried to the verandah, calling out to the kids. I silently curse to myself as I note their naked bedraggled state. This will take away precious minutes just to get them ready.

'Hey kids, come in and get dressed quickly. We are going on an adventure.'

'Where we going? Why are we going? Do we have to?' they echo in unison.

Please children, not now, I inwardly plead. I haven't the time for these endless questions in those sing-song moaning tones that children do so well. They dilly dally in, eyeing me suspiciously, annoyed at me for stopping their game. I walk briskly down the steps, trying to subtly hurry them along with gentle pushes in the smalls of their backs.

'If you get dressed super quick, we can go into town with Paula to get an ice-cream.' I'd met Paula at kinder and we quickly became friends. We had children of a similar age, and the thought of spending some time together saw the kids rush inside to get ready. 'Dry yourselves up and get some shoes and clothes on quickly. Paula will be here in a minute.'

The sound of gravel crunching on the road sends a shiver up my spine. Holding my breath as I glance out the window, I see the blue of Paula's van, just as she promised. My sigh of relief is tinged with fear. I note the watch on my wrist – thirty minutes to spare.

'Come on kids, get your shoes on. We are ready to go!' I make my voice sound full of excitement as three little children come running along the hallway, the thought of ice-cream and adventure luring them into the van.

I tighten the strap around the old suitcase, herding the children into the car. We are ready. It's time.

I stand for a precious second, glancing back at my home – a wave of emotions within my body. Desperate to hold onto the memory, this image is etched into my mind with the eye of an artist – my beautiful bush home. How I wished things were different. It became hard to swallow; the lump rose within, the tears well in my eyes. *We are going on a wonderful adventure; the children cannot see me cry.*

It will be OK, I tell myself, *I can do this. I have to keep the children safe. I need to live.*

I looked sadly at the marigolds standing in a row, waiting for the sun to bring them into colour. I remembered the day I planted them, in such anticipation of happier times. Now I wouldn't get to see them bloom. *Why am I even thinking of this? Why does it matter?*

Shaking my head as if to rattle my thoughts into place, I turn to look at Paula and smile. The van tyres start to crunch on the road. The oddly comforting sights and sound of gravel and dust allows me to breathe.

Thank you, Paula, Thank you.

2

PAULA

I'd met Paula three weeks earlier at a kinder event.

I was the newcomer in town. I knew none of the other mothers, and in truth I didn't want, nor did I wish, to make friends. Friendships would cause a whole new set of problems. I preferred life this way, being anonymous. It kept me safe. I couldn't take friends home for coffee or catch-up for a chat – they would see the truth if they became too close, they would know my secrets.

The cool breeze whispered around my shoulders as I stood back from the crowd and watched like a mother hawk whilst my son played. I secretly wished I could be anywhere but here. My eyes drifted to observe the other mothers. The movement of their lips as they chattered away seemed comically accentuated by their bright lipsticks. With their expensive heeled shoes sinking into the damp earth, and their clothing bright and fashionable, they looked out of place in this bush block setting. I glanced down at my choice of clothing, dull, drab and colourless. I wrapped my cardigan a little tighter around my aching body and felt the need to sink further into my corner. I wanted to be invisible. I hoped no one would talk to me. What would I talk about? What would I say? I was nobody.

I had stopped dressing in colour and wearing make-up many years ago. It made me look slutty, or so he said. I didn't wear lipstick. Why would I wear it with my lips? He once told me that when God handed out lips he must have thrown them at my face. They'd stuck there, skewed and imperfect. I stopped wearing lipstick from then on. I didn't want the world to see my imperfections.

'Russ, come here.'

I turned my head to see a child swinging upside down on a tree limb.

He was doing everything in his power to ignore his mother.

'Russ, come here.'

I shifted my gaze to the sound of the voice. Out of the corner of my eye I first saw Paula. Her son, the mischievous Russ, was obviously taking great pleasure in ignoring her 'secret mum language.' She was trying so hard to have her 'nice mummy' face on. I watched silently as she tried hard to attract her child's attention; all the while he continued to ignore her as he swung precariously from the tree. She was beginning to lose her patience; her words were spoken through gritted teeth and a fake smile. When she glanced up and caught me watching her, I could see the colour rising in her cheeks. As our eyes met, we both smiled. She stood out from the rest of the mums. Her dress was more casual, and her bleached white hair so vibrantly untamed.

She casually walked over to me and under her breath whispered, 'He's such a little shit.' With that, her face broke into the biggest smile. Her child was still being so wonderfully disobedient.

I couldn't help but laugh, and for a moment she was temporarily distracted from her willful son.

'I am so tired. I shouldn't have come here today. I have no patience. Oh, by the way, I'm Paula.' Her magnificent smile lit up the day.

Naughty Russ was forgotten for a while as we continued to chat about the perils of children. It was all surface conversation; husbands, children, households, general chit chat. I soon discovered Paula was also new to town and, apart from our kinder sons, we both had two younger children in tow. They had also discovered each other and were running around wildly.

Despite my reservations I had a pleasant day. Thankfully it looked like it had run its natural course as the kinder mums were beginning to disperse to their cars. I sighed with relief that I had indeed made it through the day, when I heard the words that made my senses shift to high alert, that awful numbing feeling slowly beginning to swirl in my stomach.

'Hey Jan, why don't I just take the kids home for a play?' Paula offered cheerfully. 'Let me know where you live, and I can drop them off later.'

My heart sank. *That's it, I'm trapped.* My mind raced with all the crippling possibilities that could unfold. What shall I do? I shouldn't have come to this stupid outing. I shouldn't have started talking to anyone. I should not have pretended to be normal. I've made a mistake. She's going to know. She's going to see the truth. These thoughts whirled through my mind as I carefully kept my public mask in place.

'Sure, sounds great,' I replied, and I forced that smile on my face like I didn't have a care in the world.

The children's faces beamed at me. Devon threw her soft little arms around me for a quick hug before happily waving goodbye. They ran to Paula's car with childish excitement having found new adventures, new friendships. I kept telling myself *this is normal, this is what children are supposed to do.* I waved them off with that fake smile plastered on my face.

With my pulse racing and my head throbbing, I quickly dashed to our old car to race home. I prayed that it would start first go. I had to warn him. I had to be super nice to him. I had to keep him calm and let him know. We would be having a visitor.

I could feel my heart beating hard inside my chest, its rhythmic thud reminding me to breathe. Nervously brushing my hands against my jeans to wipe the sweat clogged on my palms, I casually strolled inside to speak to him. I needed to tidy the house, something I could control – order, method, rhythm. It was in the mess I had left it that morning as I raced out the door before an argument could occur. Of course, he wouldn't clean up. He's not the woman – and cleaning, well that's woman's work.

He was sitting in his favourite chair – the daily newspapers strewn around him, beer in hand, his dope bowl and rolled up joint next to him on his table. He looked up, disinterested. He hadn't even registered the children were not with me.

'I'm just letting you know that Matthew has gone home with a new friend he has made from kinder. Devon has gone as well. The mother will be dropping them off soon and she will probably come in for a coffee. Isn't it nice they have made friends?'

My voice sounded forced. My words sounded eager to please, even to me. I hated feeling like this. Why is it always so hard?

I glanced at him to see his reaction. Nothing – OK, we will see how this plays out.

I just needed to breathe. I hated feeling so on edge all the time. What if she said something wrong? I would pay the price later. I went about my household chores, keeping a low presence, keeping everything calm. My nerves were just about at breaking point when I heard a knock on the door. The kids came running in, followed by Paula and her children. I smiled and took a deep breath.

All my senses were at fever pitch now, twitching and rippling through my body, like a deer treading gently through the forest undergrowth. I put my plastic face on, my public mask, hoping that would get me by. But I wasn't fooling anyone. I casually introduced Paula to my husband and she gave him a cheery hello. He stood up to greet her with a beer in one hand and the smell of marijuana wafting from a joint he held in the other. She seemed to take this in her stride and ignore it. I was grateful for that.

I walked into the kitchen to put the kettle on and make us a cuppa. I steered Paula in the same direction, hoping it would limit the noise of the children as well as him listening in on our conversation.

The children scampered outside to play, excited with having friends over. I was thankful for this. At least their noise would not annoy him. *Children should be seen and not heard,* he'd often say. It was a throwback to his childhood, his upbringing. I silently prayed that Paula would not say anything that would set him off, not that she would know the triggers. I hardly knew them myself.

The kettle seemed to take ages to boil as I waited to pour the coffee. All the while I kept my conversation light and carefree, my face plastered with a superficial smile belaying the abject turmoil churning inside me.

I didn't have to turn around. I could sense he had come into the kitchen. He casually sauntered to the table and took out a chair.

Oh no, here goes. I exhaled a little louder than I intended.

He engaged Paula in friendly banter and conversation, turning on the charm offensive. This was the person I once loved; so handsome, that beautiful smile, such even teeth and those laughing blue eyes. I felt sad that he had gone … was he even real? A memory flickered, a longing stirred inside me. This was all but a show, I knew that now. I watched, disconnected, as he engaged in beguiling, almost flirtatious conversation. I knew what he was doing. My face flushed crimson with the shame of it all.

So, this is how he is going to play it.

As we sat around the kitchen table I offered Paula a biscuit with her coffee. I was the perfect hostess. Paula was also being polite, watchful but polite. This intrigued me.

His warm smile reached his eyes as he continued with the conversation, focused and interested. I could feel it. I knew the mood was about to change. It's like a sixth sense I had developed. The hairs on my arms and neck would prickle like an antenna, alerting me to danger. He had started to begin a rant on politics when Paula begged to differ on one of his radical theories. I knew where this was heading. I grimaced.

Paula held her own in the conversation, refusing to be bullied or intimidated by his language and manner, as they both began to discuss the current political drama. Even though I secretly admired her bravery and intellect, I was dying inside. I kept as small and quiet as a door mouse, too scared to offer an opinion or join the conversation. I had played this scene before and I knew how it ended. I had learnt long ago not to have an opinion. I was too stupid to have one anyway, so best I kept quiet.

Suddenly he had had enough. He rose from the chair, forcefully pushing it against the table, trying to control his anger. The noise startled me into the now.

'What's to fucking eat? I need you to make me something,' he barked in my direction.

Automatically, and with survival instinct, I began to rise to prepare him something. It was the first slip up on my part. Paula saw a glimpse into my subservience.

'Can't you make your own lunch?' Paula asked with a smile on her face.

I saw his body stiffen. I felt mine do the same. We don't make those jokes in this house, we don't dare speak like that. I needed to break the moment, so I let out one of those nervous inappropriate laughs, like when someone tells a bad joke that you don't find funny, and yet everyone else is laughing. My laugh came out as a shrill giggle. I could feel it caught in my throat, mid-sound. I lowered my gaze.

He walked towards the kitchen bench, slamming cupboards and drawers, over exaggerating the noises, banging utensils around whilst making his own lunch. He started to hint rather rudely that maybe it was time for Paula to leave. I must admit there was a part of me that wanted her to go to save me this awful embarrassment. But there was another part of me who just wanted her to stay so I would be OK, be safe for a little while longer.

Paula glanced at me and once again our eyes connected. *She knows.* My shame was overwhelming.

'Can I have another cuppa? You don't mind, do you?' Paula asked him. 'The kids are playing so nicely.' Her voice was calm, polite.

He turned his head towards her, all charm and smiles again.

'No that's fine, you little women have a gossip. That's what you like to do, isn't it?'

It was said in such a belittling tone that I felt the heat in my cheeks. I knew I had turned red.

He shot me a sideways glance; I knew what that meant, too. My heart sank.

I slowly walked to the kettle and flicked the switch on ready to make another cuppa. It was going to be a long day. Paula and I sipped our coffees and talked about simple things. All the while I was aware that my responses were being listened to. He would be holding them in his memory to throw back at me. He had such an incredible mind for detail, details of no importance.

Paula eventually rose to gather her kids to go home. After a few polite departing words to him, and thanking me for the coffee, she was ready to leave. She invited me to call round anytime for a chat. I smiled at her and once again our eyes locked together.

She knows.

Paula will know I am weak and a fake. She sees behind the mask.

I walked inside, ready to clean up the collection of dirty cups. I could feel the weight of the day about to crush me. There would be consequences. He came into the kitchen.

'So, you have been out swanning around and yohoing all morning, thinking you're something you're not and you bring home a fuckin liberal dog, do you?' he roared at me.

I stiffened. Here it comes.

'I just met her today. What could I do?' It was a quiet reply.

I lowered my head, so I didn't make eye contact.

'You tell her to fuck off, that's what. You do not bring the fucking stick witch to my house – who the fuck do you think you are!' he yelled in my face, imposing his body on me.

I didn't reply. It was pointless. There was nothing I could say.

I felt the thump to my head. As I saw the arm swing again, I flinched and tried to turn away, but for some reason this always seemed to make him angrier. I never could work out why. Flinching was apparently my way of being a drama queen, provoking him. He then pounded a few more blows to my body as I tried to shield myself, trying desperately not to flinch again.

'Have you learnt your lesson now?' he asked.

I nodded my head and quietly agreed that indeed I had.

He turned away and returned to his chair. 'Now make my fucking dinner.'

The conversation was over.

Dutifully, meekly, I did as I was told. I made his dinner with order, rhythm and control whilst my silent thoughts gave me strength. *This will be over soon, I will get away from this one day*, I secretly promised myself.

My body began to ache where the punches had landed. I was sick of feeling this pain. Fortunately, the kids had continued to play outside. They had developed a handy instinct of when to keep clear. This thought saddened me even more. I was ruining their lives. I wanted to spit in his dinner, but I was not that brave.

***

It was a few days later at kinder when I again saw Paula again. She came up to me with her big smile. I had purposely been trying to avoid her at kinder drop-offs as I was so embarrassed by the events in my kitchen. As much as I would have valued a friend, I just didn't need the grief of friendship. Looking at her beaming face, it was clear I could avoid her no longer.

'Hi Chook,' she greeted me in her friendly voice. I smiled back. 'How's things?' Her eyes searched mine. 'Do you want to come to my place for a coffee?'

It was a much better option for me. He was at work today, so I would have approximately one and half hours free. I would feel less on edge at her house. He couldn't shame me if he wasn't there. I nodded my acceptance and the kids all excitedly clambered into Paula's van.

When we arrived at Paula's house the children all raced outside to play, squealing and laughing. The simplicity of children.

Paula put the kettle on. My body softened, my breathing slowed as I relaxed in her company. I felt safe. I let Paula do most of the talking. Paula wasn't intrusive – she kept the conversation light talking about herself, her family, her husband and a few juicy titbits of pre-school gossip. Paula made me laugh.

I could be her friend, I thought. *I could have a friend.*

For the next few weeks we went along like this; it became our routine. I would call into her place for a coffee on the way home from kinder and occasionally she would call into mine if we knew he would be at work. He was unsure of this new friendship, wanting to ban me from seeing her. Rather bravely I argued the point.

'It will be too difficult as we are kinder mums and the children are going to make friends as they get older. I can't just hide away. People will talk.'

He was very protective of his public image. It seemed to be well known around town that he was an A1 top bloke. He was generous to his friends and drinking buddies, charming and popular with the single ladies. He loved the footy, and the local cricket. The poor bloke just had a dragon of a wife. She was a nutcase they had heard, but he was a top bloke despite it.

Yes, he was very protective of the public persona that he had created.

I could see his mind trying to work out his plan of action, how he could manage or control the situation. When next he saw Paula, he seemed to have changed tack once again, going on the charm offensive, flirting and being over-friendly. He knew this caused me embarrassment and it was aimed to humiliate me. He had slept with every female 'friend' – and I use the term loosely – that I had made. He suggested to me rather smugly that he would be sleeping with Paula within a month.

I smiled inside. I felt this time he had met his match.

3

THE LEAVING

PART 2

The hot northerly wind, combined with 40-degree temperatures, had zapped my already depleted energy. I had no idea where I was going.

'When you get to the first destination, phone this number,' the voice on the phone had said. 'And when you get to the next destination, phone the other number.'

These were the only instructions I had been given and in an act of desperation I followed them blindly. As planned, Paula had arrived to drive us to the train station. Paula had also packed some drinks and snacks for the kids. I hadn't thought of that. I had been fraught with nerves during the drive to escape my home. *What if he sees me? His anger will erupt like a cascading volcano when he knows I've gone.*

Paula had helped to plan my escape. After a savage beating I had come asking for her help. I was tired of pretending and afraid of dying. After phoning a woman's refuge we knew what we had to do, and from there we began to plan how I could get away, how I could escape.

And so there I was, standing at the train station platform with a well-worn suitcase and three sullen looking children. Paula slipped a twenty dollar note into my hand. Squeezing it gently, she wished me luck. Tears began to well in my eyes. I was going to miss her friendship. I held her tight in an all-embracing hug as I said goodbye to my new-found friend, not knowing if I would see her again or what lay ahead. I boarded the train on my journey into the unknown.

The train's clacking rhythm moved us forward. The sounds of chattering voices were like a constant drone, the noise seeming amplified to my senses. The smell of heat and sweat seared my nostrils, suffocating me. Closing my eyes for a moment I took time to think, to breathe.

A loud noise startled me from my thoughts, and in panic I turned towards my children. My mind jolted into the now and my eyes opened wide in amazement.

Oh fuck. Gumboots. Bright pink gumboots. It's 40 degrees and she's wearing gumboots.

How had I not seen this before? In that moment Devon caught my eye. Her lip dropped, and her voice moaned, 'My feet hurting.'

'Why on earth did you put them on?' I asked incredulously. 'You haven't even got socks on.'

The bottom lip began to quiver, and the tears were ready to fall. *Please not now, I couldn't handle her two-year old meltdown.*

'I have no knickers on, too,' she wailed, and lifted her dress as if to emphasise the point.

I pulled her dress down quickly and drew her little body close to mine, but she wriggled out of my grip. The heat in the carriage was stifling. I looked towards the other passengers. Had anyone noticed? Moving across to sit with her comforter Matthew, she held his hand and gazed out the window. Tears were averted.

Why hadn't I checked what they were wearing? I was such a bad mother. What will people think? Gumboots in 40-degree heat. The swirl of panic began to rise in my throat, its bile wetting my drying mouth. *What am I doing, where am I going?* Thoughts and self-doubt begin to hammer around in my mind. The heat, the noise, the smells. I was quickly spinning out of balance, losing control.

With a relief bordering on ridiculous, I practically jump from my seat as the sound of the metal wheels come grinding to a halt on the platform. I am desperate to get the gold medal, to win the race to get off this god forsaken carriageway.

I grab my children and the suitcase. I need air.

I had no idea where I was. Everywhere people were rushing with purpose. I could feel the pull of the crowds dragging me along. The sound of shoes on concrete hammered in my head, and fumes from the trains invaded my nostrils. Voices talking constantly. So fast and loud. The anxiety starts to build in my stomach. I felt an overwhelming urge to vomit as I was consumed with fear and dread.

I needed to find a phone box and as I held my youngest child tightly by the hand, again I glanced at her gumboots. *Her feet will be so sore.* I begged Jasmine to hold her little brother's hand and stay close. Perhaps sensing my distress, they realised it was not the time to worry about girl germs.

I can't lose them in this crowd. What sort of a mother am I to do this to her children? They should all be safely at home, sitting around the kitchen table, ready for dinner, waiting to get into their pyjamas ready for bed. Waves of molten guilt washed over me.

With my spare hand I dragged my old suitcase along the station platform. Like a well-trained sheepdog I shepherd my children together through the growing throng. At the end of the platform I finally noticed a payphone. I promised the kids a cool icy pole if we could just make it there.

I dialed the first number that I was given and I'm told I must catch another train. This will be a trip of around an hour and a half. I grimace and hold in an obscenity with superhuman power. I am further instructed to ring the remaining phone number when I reach that destination, and someone will then collect me.

For a fleeting moment I wish I could crawl in a hole and cry. Living in loneliness for so long, these crowds, noises and chaos have overloaded my senses. Like a spinning top I turn in distress. *What have I done? What if I just give up, go back – or better still, what if I just give up and die somewhere? Is it worth this constant battle?* The children all look up at me confused, and I see the fear in their eyes. I know they would rather go back to the cool sprinklers of their home.

This was not the good fun adventure that Mum had promised.

What if it's all a joke? What if there is no one there at the end of the line? Rolling around in my head, these scattered thoughts create more panic. I need to stop these thoughts, I must stop them.

Squaring my shoulders, I took a deep breath, drawing in some invisible strength. I brace myself for what's ahead. This is our new life. I must remember this. We will be OK. I smile at the kids, so they believe everything is normal. This is all part of the adventure.

'Let's go on our holiday,' I say, and with those cheerful words they follow me blindly.

I scan the train timetables and find where we are meant to be. Traipsing along like a bunch of raggle taggle gypsies, we make our way to the next train. Pushed along by the crowd we find a seat. It is now peak hour and there are workers everywhere; the train is crowded. An older lady sits next to me on the seat and immediately tries to start up a conversation.

'So where are you off to, my dear?' she asks. I smile blandly – *I have no idea.*

'On a holiday,' is my curt reply. I turn my head to signal disinterest. *Please don't talk to me.* I know it's rude, but I don't want to engage in banal conversation. The dear old lady doesn't give up that easily – it's obviously a long train ride and she's up for a chat. She then focusses her attention on the little one with her squelchy pink gumboots and no knickers.

'How exciting, a holiday! Are you meeting Daddy there?'

I quietly seethe inside and shoot the poor old woman a look of pure malice. Why would you ask that? Devon looks at me, not really sure what the answer is.

'No Daddy is busy working. We are off to visit friends,' I reply.

This is more to ease Devon's mind than the nosey old woman's. I reach to hold Devon's baby soft hand, giving it a gentle squeeze to reassure her. It has been a long day and the children have been surprisingly good. The older two seem content just to stare out the window, watching the world go by. I worry what their little minds are thinking.

The train continues to rattle along, stopping at all stations. People get on and off, perspiring and sweaty in the heat. It's the hottest day of the summer and the children are now thirsty, hungry, tired and becoming restless. Having caught my eye, they begin to poke and annoy each other. Their bright red flushed faces scowl back at me for ruining their fun. Those cool sprinklers and fresh sea air back home must seem like a distant memory.

'I want to go home.' 'I want to go to the beach.' 'Where are we going?' 'Is it teatime?' They have had enough. The moaning has started. Questions, questions, questions.

The old lady looks at me. *I dare you, go on I dare you, ask me something.* My look says it all. She turns her head away to stare out the window.

Everything is bubbling up like a witch's brew in a long-ago childhood cartoon. *Bubble bubble, toil and trouble.* I am suffocating in the moment, heat, odours, pressure and questions. My head begins to spin as my stomach rumbles. Is it hunger or nerves? I should have packed more food and drink. Why didn't I think of this?

As if on cue, the announcement comes over the speaker and it is finally our stop. In panic I reach for the battered suitcase which is over my head, whilst again trying to herd three children through the throng of hot sweaty bodies and off the train. *Please don't let the doors shut on me, please stay at the platform.*

I take a step onto the platform and urge the kids to hop off, *please don't take off now with the kids on the train.* 'Jump kids, jump.' I put the suitcase down. 'Jump kids, jump.' And they do, onto the burning hot concrete platform.

Air at last – fresh air. I can breathe. The children look up at me expectantly. What now?

The bright red of the phone box is visible on the station wall and we head towards it. 'Come on kids, we are nearly there.' I try to sound excited but fear I fail miserably. I dial the number I had scribbled on a piece of paper. A calm voice answers. After explaining who I am and where I am, I silently pray there are no more trains. I am further instructed to wait where I am and that I will be collected shortly by a white van. I am so unbelievably grateful there are no more trains. After finding some water for the children and a seat to sit on in the shade, all I can do is wait. The children have been cooped up so long that they become loud and silly as they run wild at the near empty station. Finally, it is time to smile as I watch them play tag and chasey. Everything will be OK, it will all be over soon.

I notice the white van as it slowly drives into the train station carpark. It had seemed to me a long wait. The kids were still letting off steam, running around and screaming like wild bush children. Despite the disapproving looks of passersby, I was too tired to care. As a family we were all together. The van had finally arrived and that's all that mattered to me in that moment. The back door slid open. With much anticipation and trepidation, I focused my attention on a smiling woman who emerged, welcoming us in a broad Scottish accent with a cheery hello. She introduced herself as Carol. My children had stopped their game and stood together in a huddle as they eyed her suspiciously. Carol cast her gaze around the carpark. Confident that we were alone, she bundled us into the van. Finally, we were off to somewhere safe.

After a short drive through twisting streets, we came to the back entrance of a large double storey house hidden by trees. In front of us was a locked gate, which, I was informed, stayed locked at all times.

I was also told there were to be no phone calls out and no organising to meet people here. It was indeed a secret, safe location. This comforted me as I didn't want to be found.

The kids and I followed Carol inside. We were very hungry, very hot and tired. We had been on the road travelling in 40 plus degree heat for just over six hours. Carol gave us a tour around the refuge and introduced us to the other women there. We must have looked an unkempt lot. Carol guided us to our little room on the first floor. I climbed the stairs wearily. My bones and body were still bruised and aching from the pounding and beating that had caused me to flee. I was exhausted both mentally and physically. I just needed to sleep.

Another talk was given on the rules of the refuge and on other things I needed to know. The pantry was downstairs and we all helped to cook and clean. It was similar to the set up I had left in another refuge, on a previous escape attempt. *Was that really only under a year ago?*

This time I felt stronger, I had lost it all so there was nothing to lose now. Carol gave me a reassuring smile. Left alone with the children, I held my arms out and gave them all a big hug. 'This is where we will stay for a while till we can get our own house.'

Sadly, they were becoming all too familiar with these adventures. Having heard it all before, they just trusted me and went along with what I said. Looking at their little knowing faces, it seemed another piece of my heart broke. I really did need to toughen up.

'Let's have a bath, then we can find something to eat. Maybe we can find some ice cream and Milo.' And with that, they were happy to settle into our new life. So simple, really.

I found where the bathroom was and drew a nice, cool bath. I returned to our room and sat Devon on the bed as I pulled off the pink smelly gumboots. Her little feet were sore and swollen. I opened the suitcase to find what they could wear. *What had I packed?*

Unwrapping some t-shirts revealed the ceramic mugs that had the children's names boldly painted on them. Placing them gently on the bedside table, I then removed another t-shirt to reveal the ornamental china man my mother had bought me. Why had I packed these? Staring at them I shook my head. I looked for some nightwear; I hadn't packed any for them, just me.

I looked inside the suitcase. I had one pair of shorts for each child and a t-shirt. A toothbrush each, a box of hair elastics, no hairbrush, a dress each for the girls, some underwear for me and a dress for me. I could see Devon's favourite story book, Matthew's cuddly puppy and a collection of dummies. That was it.

Was that all I packed? I looked in the suitcase again, hoping something that was useful would magically appear. I sighed. I led the kids into the bathroom and told them to have a play and a wash whilst I sorted out a few things. I found Carol in her office.

'Excuse me… I didn't really pack very much, I have no nightwear or underwear for the children.' My voice was soft, apologetic.

Carol told me not to worry – they kept an extra supply as this often happened when women were fleeing their homes. I was led to a room where there was a cupboard filled with clothing of all sizes. I searched for the few items of clothing I needed, gently replacing those I did not. I found my way back to the bathroom. Knowing the children would be excited to receive some new clothes, I was able to coax them out of the bath. They were eager to dry themselves up and get ready to eat. It had been a long day. Feeling refreshed, we finally went to find some food.

It was like being the new kid in school, with everyone watching you as we walked into the communal kitchen. The women had kindly cooked us a solid meal, followed by some Milo sprinkled ice cream. After our tummies were full I thanked the women, and as the tiredness overwhelmed me we excused ourselves and finally retired to our room.

Tiptoeing across the creaky floors I finally lay on the freshly made bed with its mismatched linen. My mind began to wander. *What would he would be thinking?* He would be so angry. A shudder ran through my body and, despite the heat, I wrapped the blanket tightly around my aching bones. I was grateful for the anonymity and safety of this little house. The kids were still hot and unsettled, but we were together and that's all that mattered. They snuggled into my body as we shared the big bed; no one wanted to sleep alone tonight. I told them comforting stories.

We talked of all the things we would buy when we went shopping, when we were rich. Eventually we all fell asleep.

Day 1 of our new life was over.

The next morning, I woke in a state of confusion. As I jumped up disorientated, my body contorted with pain. Where was I? Where were my children? I looked over to see them all sleeping.

For a few precious moments I embraced this peace. Eventually they all stirred, eager and hungry to have breakfast in the communal kitchen. I made my way down the creaky stairs to find the pantry and began to make breakfast. The grinning monkey from the yellow box stared back at me. Right in front of our eyes was the biggest box of Coco Pops. The kids bounced around my feet and were beside themselves with happiness. Now this was a real treat. At this moment home seemed a distant memory. I smiled.

The workers who ran the refuge had organised to take me to Social Security to register for a pension payment. This would allow me to have some money of my own. I also needed to begin the court process. This was a scary new thing for me. The intention was to get sole custody of the children and an intervention order placed on him. This would protect me in the future. Things had now become very real. My body was churning inside, uncertain and scared. I knew he would be beyond furious that I had sided with the courts and police against him. I was now crossing the invisible line. The workers guided and supported me during this process. I was so grateful, as I would not have been brave enough to do so myself. My mind could not think clearly. I did all they asked. I listened intently as they told me what to say, where to go, what I needed to do, and I felt I wasn't alone. They offered words of encouragement as they saw me falter in fear. Yet I felt a comforting strength that someone was listening to me. They understood. I wasn't crazy, weak or making it up. I felt such overwhelming relief.

It was going to be OK.

The next day, in a cold, empty court room I was handed a piece of official looking paper. An intervention order. This impressively signed and sealed document forbade him from coming near me. As was the law, they would dutifully inform him of the events that had taken place in the court. He could of course contest them, but as I was in a safe house he could not know where I was living. This was so reassuring for me. I felt settled. I had time to think. I was safe.

As I had promised the children following on from the court appearance, we went shopping. In my hand I held my first real money. I had received an emergency cash payment from Social Security. I had never had my own money since being married ten long years ago. I felt so rich. At the refuge we paid a minimum board. The aim was to enable us to collect some savings for our future new life. I felt a rush of blood as that money sat in my hands. It was time to buy some new clothes, shoes and a few toys for the children. Carol dropped us off at the shopping centre and organised to collect us in a few hours.

It was again stressed that I was to make no phone calls or inform anyone where I was. Doing so would mean eviction from the house. There was absolutely no way I would even think of doing this. I was free.

We had the most wonderful, magical day shopping. We browsed together in shops, we had lunch in a café, we bought silly things because we could. In what seemed like a lifetime I could spend my day swinging my arms, a skip in my step, laughing, smiling, the weightlessness of not being scared or watched. It was the most wonderful day of freedom. I felt normal. The wonder and joy of this feeling was a reminder of what life could be. When Carol finally came to pick us up, the children's voices rose over each other as they excitedly displayed their shopping treats. Their wariness towards Carol had disappeared. Carol just smiled and took us home, home to our safe house.

As the weeks went by we quickly fell into the routine of living in this share house. We watched women come and go, some return to their partners, some move on to new lives. The children made friends and Jasmine finally returned to her prep year in a nearby school. We had willingly and easily drifted into a new routine. My body had healed, my mind was now clear. I felt settled. I hadn't had any word from my other life.

***

Early days after we had left, when we had the freedom to just do things. Here, a picnic in the park after shopping.

We had been at the refuge for just over six weeks when the time came for the next step. What was my plan for the future? In this time, I had grown stronger, however now I must learn to stand up for myself. It was coming time for me to move on.

I began to think of our home in the bush nestled on the clifftops of Anglesea. If I closed my eyes I could almost smell the sea air. The workers had informed me that he was being removed from the property. As public housing was only for families, he could no longer live there and it was time for him to move on. I asked about going back and having the house transferred into my name. The workers gently suggested to me that I'd need to be relocated to Gippsland, far away from where I used to live, for my own safety.

Carol told me that he had not taken the court papers well. My skin went cold.

I thought of my home. This undeniable tug, like a siren song, called me back. I had lived in my home for just over a month, after waiting and enduring so much in the time it had taken to be built. I thought of the marigolds I had planted. They would now be in bloom. My heart told me to go back there. Despite all the warnings from my rational brain, my heart and my soul called me back.

I told the workers of my decision. I was going home.

It took a few weeks to organise the relocation home. He was being removed from the lease and the property, and the lease would be transferred into my name in a straight swap over. This was all organised by the workers. I just had to sign paperwork. After all I had endured, finally I had my own home. I had my reward.

***

The day came to leave the refuge. The ladies organised a box of goods to take with me, loaded with things I would need – groceries, toiletries, information and paperwork.

The time had come to again pack my suitcase, only now I had time to think. I packed our meagre belongings carefully. I gently wrapped the three ceramic cups and the ornamental china man in pieces of clothing. As I did so, I lovingly ran my hand over them, holding them close to my heart … reminders of home.

I was going to see my marigolds. I wondered if they looked as pretty as I once imagined. I was going to smell the sweet perfume of the eucalypts in the bush, the crashing waves against the cliffs. Home to Anglesea.

We were once again bundled into the white van. This time we were going home in style, thankfully no train rides. We said our goodbyes to the women and children who had become our friends. I wished them all well, and with the biggest of smiles we were on our way.

We were going home.

4

COMING HOME

PART 1

I was coming home. After a long few weeks of planning I was finally on my way. My excitement was barely contained as I listened closely to all the things I would need to do. The intervention order was in place. It would keep me safe. I had to call the police if he came near me, the children or the house. If he broke the order he would go to jail. The thought of going home to all the things they loved, their friends, their toys, their pets, the bush, their life, had at this point sent the children into a freefall of silliness. Their excitement was contagious, and we were giddy in anticipation.

Whilst they had grown and settled in these last months, to see their natural childish enthusiasm return made me so happy. Everything would be alright.

We drove for what seemed like hours. As you enter Anglesea the trees are magically shaped into a welcoming arbor that envelope you, and the winding road lures you into a secret, special place. The children's faces beamed. The trees of Anglesea. To us it signaled home. At first, I felt it, then I heard the comforting sound of the burnt orange gravel as we drove up the hill.

It flicked and spat at the tyres on the road. As the van pulled into my driveway, I saw the marigolds all in a row, their burnt orange heads bobbing in the sunshine just as I had dreamt. My heart sang – I felt it could burst. I quickly looked around at the unkempt garden, weeds and neglect. I could fix that. Nothing could ruin my happiness.

The road home in Angelsea – as it is now and as it was then – leading up to the clifftops and bushland.

However, as I turned to the ladies with my face beaming, their faces stared back at me. They looked perplexed. They were suitably anxious when they saw the true isolation of where I was choosing to live.

'But Jan, this is a dead-end street, there's no-one around. You are so isolated.'

Uncertainty began to weave its threads through my body. I surveyed my surrounds and tried to see it through their concerned eyes. All I felt and saw was peace and quiet, a wonderful expanse of heathland and space. A twinge of doubt and fear ran through my body like a small electric shock. I nervously looked around to make sure I wasn't being watched from behind a tree or bush. My inbuilt antenna buzzed. I was getting spooked. *It will be OK ... I will be safe.*

The ladies handed me the keys to my home. Finally, I stepped inside.

There was no furniture. The kitchen table was gone – so, too, was the lounge suite.

The kids ran to their rooms. There were no beds, no drawers, clothes or toys. No pet dog. The children looked to me confused. Where were their things? Was this the home they left? As I rolled my head in despair, I looked up and noticed no lightbulbs. In every room the lightbulbs had been taken out – all the furniture gone, everything I once had was taken. Clothes, photos, trinkets and treasures ... all removed. What do I do now? Why would he do this to the children? Deep in my heart I knew. He was making a statement.

Sighing deeply as I sat on the floor, I again felt the invisible blanket of despair wrap around my body like an English fog. We had no TV, no music. Where was the fridge? The workers looked at me saddened and shocked at my dismay. They couldn't stay to fix this; they had to leave and return to their work, I knew this. It was time for me to stand on my own.

Again, they gave me a list of do's and don'ts. They asked me to be careful, take no risks, and handed me a list of phone numbers. I gave them a brave smile. I would be OK, everything would be OK.

Outside, the marigolds were bobbing in the sunlight.

We had a house, our home. We would start again.

I hugged the women and thanked them for helping to rebuild my life. Their quiet confidence and belief was a soothing balm to my broken mind and spirit. They had allowed me the space and safety to think clearly and to plan ahead ... but now it was time to say goodbye.

I led them outside. I gazed up to the sky in a silent prayer of thanks, catching a glimpse of the TV antenna, or what should have been a TV antenna. It was totally dismantled. The pieces were strewn all over the garden. I began to laugh, a manic demented kind of laugh as I noted the irony. I didn't have a TV, so this didn't really matter.

Little did I know it was just the beginning of a new game.

5

THE GAME

PART 1

Since returning from the refuge, I had been back in Anglesea for around a week when I heard the sound of fire engines. Living in the bush and a high fire risk area, this was always a concern. I had made a fire plan and had put together a fire escape box, but basically my plan was to just run away at the first opportunity. Bravery has never been my strong point.

The sound of the fire engines seemed to be getting closer. The smell of smoke hung heavily in the air. I ventured outside with some trepidation to see what was happening and if I needed to take some form of action. As I heard the sirens' wail get louder, the thought occurred to me that I could be in danger.

A wave of slight panic rose in the pit of my stomach as I realised the tea trees close to the walking track were on fire. Thankfully the older children were at school and kinder, but I was alone with a small child and no vehicle. What should I do? We would have to make a run on foot. Could I outrun a fire? With only Devon at home, it would make escape easier.

For a few fleeting seconds I was transfixed in fear, trying to think of a plan. The urgency of the siren sound jolted me into action. I raced inside to find the fire box, removing woolen jumpers, strong shoes and a woolen blanket. I grabbed my little girl. It was time to run.

Where were the fire brigade? I could hear their sirens so they must be close by, but where were they? I grabbed Devon's tiny hand and raced outside. I continued to look anxiously down my street, willing them to come along and put out the fire. With the deepest sigh of relief, I saw a flash of red as the fire engines raced across the bush fire tracks. Devon and I stood sweltering in our heavy woolen jumpers and sturdy shoes in the middle of the road, watching as the fire was quickly extinguished. Devon was enjoying the colour and excitement – what a story to tell her siblings. Myself, I was just thankful a disaster was averted.

We stripped off our heavy jumpers and shoes and Devon returned inside to play her games. I sat quietly on my front porch, relieved that the drama was over. Closing my eyes to feel the warmth of the sun's rays on my face, I was idly daydreaming when a noise distracted me from my thoughts. Like a startled rabbit I opened my eyes, and to my complete shock I saw him approach me.

I was rooted in fear. In that moment all my brave thoughts and strong self-talk dissolved in an instant. Old habits die hard and I looked around for the kids. *Where were they, were they safe?* He approached the driveway, his walk sharp and purposeful. My pounding heart called me to action as I slipped over my own feet, flailing towards the door. Slamming it shut and locking it tight, I sent Devon to play in her room to keep her out of the way.

His first words were gentle and soft. He was so charming, so nice. He told me how much he missed me, how he had changed, how he missed the kids, how lonely he was. With a grand gesture he produced a beautiful blue sapphire ring sitting in a heart-shaped box. He had purchased this just for me, so we could get back together.

Futile words and gestures, cascading onto a stone heart. My resolve was strong. I politely asked him to leave and reminded him rather primly that he wasn't allowed near me or the property. We had court orders in place. Strangely at this point I did not contact the police. I foolishly believed that I, with the courts' backing, had the power to make him leave. My signed, red sealed and stamped crisp white document would surely make him see reason. He would not want to be in trouble with the courts or go to jail.

His charm then turned to outright venom and anger.

'How do you like watching TV?' he asked.

I did not respond.

'So, you have some new friends in a white van, have you? Are they your lesbian friends telling you what to do? I saw you come back, thinking you're all good and smart.'

The coldness trickled through my body. He had been watching me. My antenna was right. Where had he been hiding? Again, I did not respond.

'It's a shit fire brigade you've got there. Don't think they are going to save you if you were really getting burnt out. It took them 5 minutes to get here and they went down the wrong street, they don't even know how to get here. You are pretty lucky it was only a test fire – if I had done it for real you would be burnt out,' he stated as a matter of fact. 'You should be grateful I have given you the chance to see how incompetent they are. They're not going to help you, neither will your courts or your coppers.'

It slowly dawned on me that it was him who had started the fire.

'Did you do that? Did you start the fire?' I asked incredulously.

He just smirked at me. 'Can I come in?' he asked. 'We need to talk.'

'You must leave. I am ringing the police.' I made my way to the kitchen where the phone sat on the wall, giving him a clear view of me as I made the call.

He then started to bang on the windows with his clenched fists. The glass rattled and shook. I was fearful it would break. He began to yell a torrent of abuse, calling me horrible names, all the while threatening to kill me if he got hold of me. That old feeling of fear began to produce the sickly bile in my throat. My hands shook as I dialed the number of the local police. I just prayed he wouldn't be able to break in.

As he saw me on the phone talking to the police, he went ballistic. 'You are a give-up dog, a lagger and you know what happens to give-ups and friends of the police.' He smashed the window again with his fist for effect; it rattled precariously. I stared at the glass, willing it with cosmic powers to stay strong and in one piece. He then turned and left.

The police finally arrived a good thirty minutes later. By this time Devon was shaking and upset, clinging to my leg in fear. Her soft little eyes welled with tears as I held her close to comfort her, stroking her cheeks to let her know it would be OK. I was again taken back to a time when I felt powerless by the onslaught of abuse and violence. Lightning bolts of hatred. Shards of words and force from a fire-spitting, vengeful dragon.

I had enjoyed a week of quiet and had been lulled into a false sense of security. I had let my guard slip. I must never do that again. It wasn't over. The game had changed.

When the police arrived, I began to explain what had happened. My words were spilling out between deep breaths, my hands flew wildly for dramatic effect, my voice shook. With great drama I told them he had started the fire to burn me out, how he had banged at the windows and threatened to kill me. The policeman stood there impassively. *Maybe he, too, had heard the stories about the nutcase that lived on the hill.* 'Where is he?'

'He just walked away,' I replied.

'Where does he live?' the policeman asked.

'I don't know,' I replied quietly.

'Is he driving a car?' he continued.

'I didn't see one. I don't think so.' I remembered my initial shock at seeing him just appear.

'What do you want us to do?' he asked. 'He isn't here now.'

I looked at him. *I don't know,* I thought. *Just make him stay away. Keep me safe.*

The policeman had a quick look around, opening the gate to the backyard, poking his head in the shed and gazing disinterestedly towards the bushland. He surmised there was not much he could do as it seemed my ex had already gone. 'Just call us again if he comes back.' And with that they left.

I stood there bewildered. *Is that it?* My feet felt like I was walking in quicksand as I returned inside. I cuddled Devon, again reassuring her we were OK, sending her back to her room to continue her game. The weariness engulfed me as I lay down on the lounge room floor, gazing up at the white of the ceiling. I needed to think.

I felt it at first. My sixth sense, my intuition. I sat up and he was at the window, watching me. I jumped up like a startled cat.

'Stupid fucking coppers,' he yelled. 'I was in the bushes all the time. You can't rely on them, you know. You're fucked, 'cause I'm going to kill you. You won't know where or when, but you're fucked.'

With that he turned and left.

I stayed on the floor. With my head in my hands I finally cried. Would it never end?

How the hell did I get to this?

Memories came flooding back from years ago, from the beginning. Had it all just started from a detour on a trip to the beach? Was that all it took to change the course of my life?

Like a fractured homemade movie my life unfolded, projected before me onto a blank screen of the white ceiling above – all the memories to bring me to this moment …

6

IN THE BEGINNING

It would always be the seasons that conspired to change the course of my life, sliding door moments that change the course of who you are and all you believe.

In the summer of 1971, as a gawky fourteen-year-old, I was unsure of myself. Like many of my peers, I was looking to fit in, find my place in this big world I was beginning to discover around me. I had dreams that I could be anything I wanted to be, unaware of the reality of life. I was ready for romance, fun and mischief. In that delicious summer of school holidays, long lazy days and balmy evenings were spent listening to the many pop songs on the radio, dancing to Slade or doing the Eagle Rock. There were days frolicking at the beach, yet never going for a surf or swim, or hanging around the local Bombora milk bar catching up with my group of friends.

This was our entertainment in the small country town where we lived in. I was never brave enough or cool enough to join in with the cool kids. They were the ones who went in cars with boys, dressed in surfie clothes, had their hair bleached blonde by the sun and bodies tanned from days spent surfing and swimming. I was more the red hair, pale English skin and freckles-type, covered up from the sun's harsh rays.

On these hot summer afternoons, the searing heat would burn through my leather sandals whilst I watched the mirage of colours shimmering and dancing in waves from the concrete pavement. As the blowflies buzzed around my head, I would attempt to swat them away. My throat was often dry and parched from the air of the north wind, and I would search for the nearest garden hose to wet my lips.

On this particular scorching January day, one of the boys in our gang, Simon, promised us he could load us up with cold drinks if we tagged along with him. The plan was to detour from our proposed beach adventure to quickly call by his house. His older brother had arrived home from the Merchant Navy and was all cashed up. In an effort to impress us all, he was certain he could source some money from his brother for milkshakes, cool drinks and lollies. As he was willing to share with us, the offer was eagerly accepted. In those endless summer days, we had nowhere else to be in a hurry.

How different could my life have been if I had said no?

As we all lounged on the front lawn, our friend Simon raced inside to get the money. Laying on the cool grass in my tiny denim shorts and bikini top, I aimlessly picked at bindies and dry blades of grass, languidly soaking up the sun's rays, sunning my oh so white legs and body. I was idly waiting for Simon to return with his booty when I noticed someone emerge from the house. My teenage heart skipped a beat and all the girls sat up and stared.

He resembled one of the many rock star posters I still had on my bedroom wall with his long hair and tattoos. He was shirtless with suntanned skin and a muscular body. He looked nothing like the boys we hung out with. I continued to stare at him, mouth agape, until I realised he was coming up to me. *Me.*

Out of the group of girls that were sitting there preening and posing, staring at him, he came up to me. With teenage awkwardness I blushed and shuffled into what I hoped looked like a casual position. All the while my heart was pounding. *What do I say? What should I say?* I wanted to act cool.

'Hello flower,' he said. 'What are you doing today, beautiful?'

He called me beautiful. He held out a hand to help me get up and I could feel my cheeks burning. I could feel everyone staring at me and was trying desperately to appear nonchalant. He smiled at me and I suspect he knew what he was doing to me. He stroked the side of my face with his hand.

My stomach fluttered, and my heart raced so fast I thought everyone could hear its pounding. I was enchanted.

My friends soon grew bored with this display and wanted to get on with their day, indicating it was time to leave. Giving me a nudge along they grabbed me by the hand and we continued on our way. I turned my head and snuck in one last look. He was watching me.

As the summer of 1971 progressed I seemed to see him often. He would always seek me out from the group and ask to spend time just hanging out with him. It seemed I was the chosen one. As fickle as a youthful heart is, I was happy to ditch my group of friends to do just that. Within a few short weeks I felt I needed to act more grown up, so it was no more childish parties or beach games. No more hanging around milk bars, flirting with boys and developing my seductive guile. I had scored the jackpot. I had a grown-up boyfriend and he just wanted to be with me.

I soon learnt that he was only home for a short while as his job was working at sea several months at a time. If he was going away again to sea, I decided I must spend all my time, every minute, with him.

My father, however, was not impressed. The fact he was four years older than me and a 'man of the sea,' my father considered him too worldly for me. The fact that my parents disapproved of him added a touch of wickedness and teenage rebellion to the romance. This put me in conflict with them. I considered myself a rebel. I was definitely cool now.

After a few weeks the time came for him to return to his job at sea. I knew he had to leave. I was heartbroken. I thought that he would never come back. Maybe he would forget me, find someone else, someone better, older, smarter. My teenage doubts were laid to rest when just prior to him leaving he presented me with a gift – a gold friendship ring. I was now officially his girlfriend.

'That's to make sure you don't see other boys. You're mine now,' he said lovingly whilst placing the ring on my finger.

He loves me so much, he chose me.

I flaunted that ring around like a trophy. It was my suit of armour for any amorous young teenage boys who may have fancied me. Not that they had ever done so before, but now it was bad luck if they did. I had a boyfriend, I was chosen.

How silly was I?

Whilst he was away at sea, every week I would get a letter declaring his love. Every now and then I would get a telegram from some distant port, professing his love. He would ask many times if I was still his girl and what I had been up to? He loved me so much. Even when he was away, he thought of me.

I no longer felt part of our gang. I had moved on, as had they.

As the seasons changed, this became my way of life. He would go to sea, and I would await his return. Each time my life would be on hold, just waiting. He would return and shower me with love and gifts.

My Dad would encourage me to go out, visit friends, go to parties, try new things whilst he was away at sea. But I churlishly refused, and would just sit at home and wait for him to come home to me. When he did return from the sea, Dad would place time limits on when and where I could see him. Dad tried all sorts of ways to break us up, but a teenage heart is foolish, rebellious and strong.

At times, encouraged by him, I would break the rules and stay out late. I'd do things I knew I would be in trouble for. I would constantly question and challenge my parents' authority. I was in love; did they not understand this?

Around a year into the relationship, I was surprised when just prior to him leaving again he presented me with an engagement ring. A glittering sparkly diamond in a delicate gold band.

I was fifteen.

Full of my own importance and in love, I of course accepted the ring and it dazzled and glittered on my finger for all the world to see.

I was treated like a queen, lavished in gifts. I belonged to only him. He talked of marriage and the need to get away from the control of my parents. Any problems or arguments we did seem to have were because my parents weren't letting us do what we wanted. I understood that. I believed it. I became a willful, disobedient brat.

My parents were furious.

During this time, there were signs that caused me to sometimes question what I was doing. Unlike my parents, I did not have the maturity or wisdom to see a pattern of behaviour. His obsession was love to me. His control was love to me. Everything was done for love, his love of me.

At times I saw glimpses of his temper, but I believed this was caused by me. I would be heartbroken if he yelled at me.

'You're only a girl; don't act like a child,' he would tell me. 'You have to learn to grow up.'

I had made him angry when I had spoken to a boy I used to know from my schooldays. He was furious. He was going to leave me there and then for flirting around and disrespecting him. Even though I knew I was just talking to a boy, I still apologised and said it would never happen again.

'You are mine, just mine, you belong to me,' he would say. *He loves me so much* is what I would hear.

I didn't want to make him angry. It scared me. I had to change. I would try to be a better girlfriend so he would not yell at me. I would try harder to be a grown up, to not act like a child.

In the summer of 1973, just after I had turned sixteen, he asked me to marry him. I of course said yes, but my father said no. My response was to run away from home when I felt like it, or not come home on time, staying out till all hours of the night. I was doing what I wanted, what we wanted. I became disruptive and disobedient and would sulk and cry, till eventually I wore my parents down. When my father sat me down and asked if we were having a sexual relationship and I confirmed we were, he finally said yes. I recall the words my mother said at the time. 'You have made your bed, now you have to lie in it.' Finally, I had my own way.

I was so happy. No more having to come in at 9:30pm on weekends. No more rules. I could do what I want. I would be married. This was the still the time when to have a child out of wedlock was still considered shameful. My parents were concerned this could happen, and so finally agreed to a January wedding.

His behaviour changed somewhat in the lead up to the wedding. He was getting angrier at small things. When I suggested something I would like for the wedding, he would become dismissive. He had it all organised.

I dreamt of a pretty white dress and veil, like I had seen women wearing in Mum's magazines. I would be surrounded by flowing benevolent bridesmaids in gowns of lilac. Sadly, it occurred to me I had no friends who could play this role. Secretly I wanted the fairytale wedding, however I didn't speak up or say anything. I knew he would see it as childish. He had it all under control, he had chosen my outfit.

I began to feel stabs of uncertainty, and wanted to change my mind and run away just weeks before the wedding. But now things had been put in place and it was spiraling out of my control. I soon came to understand it was not a childish game. This was not a fairy tale, it was serious grown up business. Other people were now involved doing things; there were legal obligations. People were expecting a wedding.

He had found us a flat to live in and organised all the furniture and fittings so that we could move in straight after the reception. He had organised absolutely everything; what we would wear, who could come, what colour furnishings and style 'we' would have in our home. What food we would fill the cupboards with. Everything was done. I just had to be there.

It was all happening for real. I was frightened. I wanted it all to stop, but I didn't know how.

If I wasn't so pigheaded and ashamed of my behaviour I could have spoken to my parents. But I didn't want to admit that maybe I was wrong.

It was no big fancy wedding for us. No beautiful white wedding dress. I wore a bright red pinstripe pantsuit. There was no church or grand walk down the aisle. Just a registry office with faceless people and cold stone walls. The reception, for want of a better word, would be coffee and cake at my parent's home, served on the good china. It was only family in attendance. No one dressed up, no decorations were on display. It seemed this was not a wedding to celebrate.

1974. Yes, this was what I got married in. It was chosen for me.

After the reception we headed to what would be our new home. I was now a married woman. The honeymoon was over before it had begun. I had no idea why he was angry, but he was furious about something. He yelled and screamed and would not let me sleep in our bed. I was told to go sleep on the couch. I sat there bewildered. This was not how it was meant to be.

1974 – just married. My greatest wish was to stay out later than 9.30 on weekends and do what I wanted – how silly was I?

What had happened? What had I done? I had very little sleep that night. I was so upset and just cried. I couldn't go back to my parents – that would have been too embarrassing. I had nowhere to go. I was stuck. I felt so small, so alone.

The next morning, he woke up full of apologies. I received flowers, chocolates and lots of 'sorrys'. He explained to me what I had done to make him angry. And I of course agreed I would not do it again.

The pattern had been set without me knowing it.

It was three weeks after we were married that he left again to go to sea. This time he would be away for three long months. In my heart I was so very happy. I needed a break, I needed a rest. There was a big part of me that was thankful he was gone. I could live by myself and do whatever I wanted until he returned. Maybe the time away would make me miss him and love him again. Finally, freedom. In effect I felt I could have the best of both worlds. I thought that maybe this was quite a clever solution to living my life.

Whilst he was away I continued to receive telegrams asking what I was doing, who I was seeing. Did I miss him? I had at this time started to work in a factory with my mother. She thought I needed to earn my own money and it would also give me something to do. I enjoyed this new freedom and having some money of my own. Occasionally I would catch up with my new work friends and go out. I began to purchase things I liked for our little flat and decorate it with trinkets I wanted. I ate whatever I fancied, which was mainly ice cream with chocolate topping and crushed nuts. I began to embrace this lifestyle. This newfound happiness and independence was obviously reflected in my voice. He detected it when he called, and it made him angry. He felt I was not missing him enough. Strangely I wasn't.

Three months later he arrived home from sea to tell me he had officially resigned to spend his time with me. He couldn't bear to be away from me again. This was not what I wanted or expected. This was not part of my new plan.

He asked me to quit work to be home with him all day. After all he had given up the sea for me, it was the least I could do for him, right? Regretfully I quit my job and said goodbye to my new friends. I had lost my independence.

He never worked another day for the next four years, choosing to be with just me – him and I in our cocoon. I was isolated, controlled and trapped.

What had I done?

7

COMFORTABLY NUMB

In the winter of 1976 it was hard to believe that three and half years prior I had still happily been playing with my Cindy dolls and pretending to be a teacher to my toys. Although I would never admit it to my friends, I still slept with my security blanket. Every Sunday night I would settle in front of the TV with much anticipation as the stories would unfold on *Disneyland*. My Mum would lovingly brush my long hair, the strokes rhythmic, soothing, whilst I would eat my raspberry jam sandwiches and dream of all the possibilities of a wonderful life when I lived in my own fantasyland.

This time seemed so long ago. I was now pretending to be an adult.

This was not quite the image I once had in my head of a grown-up life. I thought I would have someone to love and adore me forever. I would play house and surround myself with things that I thought were special and beautiful. My childish dreams had definitely not gone to plan. And I had no idea how to make it better, how to change it. So here I was. I had become so tired of waiting for the fantasyland dream that I had to find other options to get me through my miserable days.

You've made your bed, now you lie in it. The words of my mother would often ring in my ears.

In these early years, he was not extremely physically abusive towards me – at least not by what I would later have to gauge this against. The late seventies were still the time of *sorry*, apologies and flowers after he slapped me around. The emotional and psychological abuse was deeper and ever so subtle until I realised too late that I had a problem that I could not fix or escape from.

After he had given up working at sea, his time was now spent at home with me. Drugs were then introduced into my lifestyle. I had not really noticed this before, or maybe I was too ignorant to know better. Drugs and alcohol were a constant in his life. It was only a matter of time before drugs became a constant in mine. After my first tentative steps of smoking dope, I soon discovered drugs became a way for me to become comfortably numb. I could block myself from reality and quiet the constant questions in my mind. Drugs became my form of denial when it all became too hard. I just let it happen. I had found my escape.

I began to spend my days smoking dope, with minimal effort and caring put in to functioning at all. Long endless days lay ahead, and I would laze in bed too stoned to bother getting up. If I bothered at all, the comfy chair would be my goal where meaningless television shows would grab what limited attention I had. Listening to music from his extensive record collection would send me into a dizzying head space, where again I would have to lay down from the intensity of it all. There was no pop music in our house; it was all layered noise. We were cut off from the world. It was just us in our little drug bubble.

In the mid-seventies cocaine was relatively easy to access in Australia. I was given a taste of this new drug. Cocaine gave me a feeling of bravado, of courage and excitement. It made me happy. I had found my 'thing'. I began to use it regularly over a period of a few weeks. If I did not have a sufficient supply, agitation would set in. To him I was becoming a problem, I had become uncontrollable. The one good thing I thank him for at this time is that he cut my supply and refused to have it in the house. However, I suspect this was more for his benefit than my wellbeing. For me, I simply returned to my zoned-out dope smoking phase where nothing really inspired me.

I was again comfortably numb.

In late 1976 we were living in an orchard in a small seaside town. As with most houses we rented, they tended to be in coastal towns and isolated from people, services and family. The house was set on acreage and it was covered in by trees and foliage, not visible to prying eyes. Its darkness held an air of disquiet. There was a piano next to the bay windows, which I loved. I would walk by and tinkle the keys. A wonderful old brick fireplace took up the centre of the room; the ceiling beams were low and dark. Even in the summer I would light the open fire each day to stare at the flames and colours and bring warmth into the house. There were the usual assorted group of 'friends' that would call around occasionally, but it was mainly a drugged out, isolated lifestyle.

It came as a complete shock to me to discover I was around five months pregnant. At the time I was recovering from anorexia and assumed I would not be able to fall pregnant, nor was I planning to. The guilt I felt was painful. What had I been doing to myself, my body, my baby?

This new life inside me would be the catalyst for change. He must get a job, be responsible. It was time for the *Disneyland* happy family I had once dreamed of. No more dope smoking or drugs. I had a focus. Slowly and surely, I began to see with clear eyes that there was a world to live in and a life to live. I would have a child, responsibility. The baby would need things, cots, nappies, clothing, security, love. A warmth and energy lit up my body, excited to become a mother. It was time to dream and plan all the things that would change.

The cracks really started to appear as he continued with a lifestyle I was ready to leave behind. I wanted to grow up. I started to find my voice and ask for changes in how we lived. He needed to get a job, we needed to buy things to prepare for the times ahead. I started to question his authority.

The beginning of the first ending would arrive on Good Friday 1977, weighing 6lb 2 oz. A healthy little girl, my beautiful Jasmine. I was 20 years old.

8

CONTROL, ISOLATION, SHAME, LOATHING

On finding out I was pregnant we had moved from the dark, isolated orchard drug house. He decided we would live in a caravan at his parent's house. This thought filled me with dread. The plan was to save money to buy our own house.

As the due date of the birth was looming closer, we had nothing prepared for the baby's arrival. In the cramped confines of the caravan whilst cooking him dinner, I meekly broached the subject again of asking for money to buy what we needed for the baby; basic items, blankets, nighties, nappies. We had nothing. He lost his temper and, whilst screaming at me for my neediness, he swung his hand out, slapping me across the face. I fell back on the caravan seat, the smell of stale beer and warm stew adding to my feelings of nausea and despair.

My humiliation no longer seemed so important, so I called my dad to come and collect me and I moved back home. My parents took such gentle care of me. My mum took me shopping and we bought little nighties and singlets for the baby. I ran my hands over the delicate clothing – so white and soft I had to nuzzle my face into them. Mum took me into her bedroom and, with great pride, produced a little box covered in soft tissue paper, smelling of lavender. Inside was a collection of all the booties and matinee jackets she had been knitting in matching layettes. My parents even bought me some comfortable maternity clothes as I had been wearing my old clothes which stretched across my growing belly. I began to look and feel like a mother.

I secretly could have stayed there forever getting spoilt and cared for, however, with four siblings in a three-bedroom house, it was very crowded. It seemed I was forever dodging my younger brother's toys on the lounge room floor, or listening to a cacophony of differing music sounds coming from the bedrooms. Dinner times were spent squashed around the crowded table, against the backdrop of the multi-coloured wall paper my dad was so proud of. The constant fights over whose turn it was to do the dishes. It seems I had forgotten how to live as a family.

Meanwhile, *he* began making all the right gestures of apology and begging for forgiveness, calling around at my parents' house looking stylish, hair combed back, clean shaven and carrying a bunch of flowers. He would make his way to the lounge room and the family would disappear to offer us some private time. My siblings would pull faces behind his back and I would try to stifle a giggle. I would sit on the well-worn chairs and pick at the stitching around the edge, something I had done as a child, here, when I was part of the family. In my naivety and the childish dream of happy families, at the time I believed him. My father gave him a stern talking to, threatening he would wear the consequences if he ever hit me or touched me again. I wanted to believe it would be OK. Surely he would change when a baby was here. Reluctantly I went back to him.

I'd made my bed, I had to lie in it. There was a baby on the way. We had to work it out.

My father passed away unexpectedly six months after his beloved first granddaughter Jasmine was born. In deep shock, weighed down by guilt and grief, my heart ached. My pain was intense as I mourned for my father. I knew I had let him down with my life choices. I deeply regretted the grief I had caused him in my teenage years. I would never get the chance to say how truly sorry I was, and admit that I was wrong.

The physical violence escalated only days after my father was gone. I had no time to wallow in pity or grief. I soon came to realise that I had no one to protect me now. I was alone.

How did it come to this? How had this happened? This question haunted me.

Many years later I would still search for the answer. I am not sure I have ever found it.

Until being with him, I had not witnessed family violence or violence of any kind. I didn't know it existed. As a child I would watch my parents. I just knew they loved each other. My parents would dance together, laugh at secret jokes with that special look they had just for each other. When my father came home from work he would rest his head on my mother's lap at night. She would gently stroke his hair. Naturally our family had the usual arguments and fights, but it was about nothing things. Who watched what on TV? Who had pinched the toy from the cereal packet? Who had cheated at Monopoly? When my Dad had snuck to the pub and stayed a bit too long, you would hear him coming home singing songs from half way down the street. I would hear Mum scolding his behaviour with her slightly raised angry voice. We kids had heard that voice lots of times and we knew Dad was in trouble. Even though Mum had been angry, it was always resolved by the next day. It somehow had seemed to be sorted out, usually with my Dad singing more songs to my annoyed mother. No one hit or hurt anyone to make their point or win the argument.

How do you hurt someone you say you love? Why would you hurt someone? I just couldn't understand this. Why would you intentionally cause pain to someone?

Over the years I often doubted myself and wondered. *What did I do? Was it me?* Maybe I was stupid, maybe I didn't understand things. I became confused as to what was happening and why. Maybe I did overcook the potatoes. Maybe I did wash his clothes wrong. Maybe I didn't understand instructions. I would try to concentrate and listen harder. Maybe I could have been a better housewife. I should have tried to keep the house tidy, cook better meals, clean up the sink. Maybe I wasn't a 'dutiful' wife who'd have sex on demand. Maybe I did love the kids more than him, pay them more attention. I used to believe all of these maybes. I needed to know and understand what was wrong with me. Why did he hit me? Why did he hurt me? Why did this pain happen to me?

It must have been my fault, as I knew no one else it happened to.

***

In the ensuing years I found it easier not to see my family to protect myself from their pitiful, scornful looks. I protected myself from their disgust at my weakness. I was invited to fewer family functions and events. It would mean inviting him and he always managed to start a fight or embarrass me or, worse, my family. If he wasn't going, then he would not allow me to go to any family event on my own.

As my sister's wedding approached in the late summer of 1978 I knew that I would be unable to attend. He had spent the weeks leading up to the big day threatening what he would do at the event. He would shame me and my family. He was rather pleased to watch my distress when he spoke of how he would ruin her day. I desperately wanted to go, but the risk was too high. If I had gone by myself, I would have worn a few black eyes to match my dress. I couldn't go. I paid the price of this decision within my family for many years. I had chosen him over them. I missed many family events, as it all became too hard.

I made up many stories to hide the reasons behind the bruises and injuries. I stopped going places, hiding at home where I could be invisible. If no one could see me, no one would ask. No one would know. I was so ashamed and embarrassed at my failures, my weakness, that I wanted to keep it a secret.

1979. Me with Jasmine and pregnant with Matthew.

I became a good liar. There was the time I had my nose broken. We were living in a dreary little house in yet another isolated town. At this time Jasmine was a two year old toddler and I had a new four month old baby, our first son Matthew. The house was cold and drab and I wanted to freshen it up and keep it warmer by putting up some new curtains. I just could not reach the right spot, so reluctantly had to ask him to help. With much annoyance, muttering under his breath, he slammed the door as he went outside to get the ladder. *Maybe I should have just kept quiet,* I pondered as I rushed towards the door to let him in. He shot me a dark glance, the hairs on my arms twitched and I shuddered. He was in a mood now. As he started to climb the ladder balancing the curtain fitting in one hand, I offered to hold the ladder steady. He could not reach the required height. Instead of moving the ladder again, he over reached and nearly fell. This of course became my fault. Who was the one who wanted to put up new curtains? What a 'stupid needy bitch' I was.

As he began to climb down from the ladder, my concentration was intent on holding it safely so he wouldn't fall. Next minute a thumping back hander knocked me off my feet. The pain was instant as I heard the breaking of bone, the taste of blood in the back of my throat. Tears welled in my eyes as I tried to take a breath in, but I was breathing in pain. The blood fell from my face, dripping onto my top, mixing in with baby vomit and breast milk stains.

As I looked up I saw shock on his face. I knew then that something was wrong. With the swagger of a punch-drunk prize fighter, swaying my way to the bathroom I started to clean up the blood and see what damage had been done. I could feel it. My nose was well and truly broken. I could see the kink of the break in the top half.

What would people think? How could I hide my face? The cover story was already formulating in my mind, the criminal working on her alibi. How could I go out in public looking like this? Looking forlornly at my battered face in the mirror, my reflection questioned: was that really me? Is this who I was? I was a mess. Gently dabbing away the blood, I knew this time I needed to get to a hospital. A broken nose – well of course a door slammed into it, really it did.

Snapping back to the present – I now gently ran my hand across the bridge of my nose. The kink is still there. As I lay on the floor of my empty lounge room wallowing in my sadness and reflecting on the past, I could hear Devon playing happily in her room. Had it all been worth it, all the lies of the past? Would the truth have kept me safe? Every bruise, every scar had a story, and each one more unbelievable than the last. I thought of all the cover stories I had told over the years – all the moments, the plans, the deals with the devil that led me to here, and to the final opportunity to leave. And yet, after this morning's tirade at the window, I still didn't feel safe or confident that it was all over. Staring at the ceiling, it seemed I was lost in a warped nostalgia of ten long years.

I remembered the story I'd told the doctors and nurses at the hospital all those years ago. I still quietly cringe at the total implausibility of this happening. I remember the pain as my nose was pushed back into place, and the start of the bruising spreading up to reveal two big black eyes. I wanted to die of shame. Hospital was always my last resort. I preferred to heal in private, so no one could see what I had become. It was my fault, I was so ashamed.

Years later, I found myself again in need of hospital assistance after a severe beating.

As usual, I had unintentionally caused him to be angry. Jas had just started school and I often envied the mothers so nicely dressed at the school gates. I would walk to collect her, scurrying in so no one would notice me. Deciding to cheer myself up, I wanted to look nice for a change, instead of looking like the *drab sack of shit* he says I always looked like. Putting on a nice pair of jeans, I did my hair up in a different style and added a dash of makeup. That made me feel better and I stood a little taller as I entered the lounge room.

Believing in his mind there must be an ulterior motive for this sudden makeover, he deduced that, of course, I was having an affair. I was planning on leaving him. Why else would I do this?

I ignored his baiting and sat myself in the comfort of the maroon club chair, surveying the lounge room for nothing in particular. He leapt up, gripped the arms of the chair, bending over me whilst screaming insults and vitriol in my face. *'Slut, whore, bitch. Who do think you are?'* His anger was so blind he grabbed his beer bottle from the nearby table and swung it at my face, intending to scar me. In a perfect reflex response, I raised my knee to shield the blow and protect my face, curling my body tightly into a protective ball. A captured animal knowing its fate, waiting for the inevitable onslaught. The bottle smashed against my knee, causing the brown glass splinters to be embedded in the blue denim and into my skin. I continued to bleed from a hundred little fragments, the brown shards now lost in the deep red of blood.

A trip to the hospital was needed to remove the glass splinters and stem the blood loss. The slightest movement of glass under my skin caused me pain, so he had to drive me to hospital, dropping me off at Emergency to walk in alone. It was time for another made-up story about my injuries which was totally unbelievable, and probably physically impossible, but I stuck to it, and could feel the disdainful disbelief of the nurses and doctors as they fixed me up. I was a liar; we all knew it.

I just needed to get home to the children – they had been frightened and cowering in the kitchen when they heard the yelling from their father; their eyes had widened when they saw blood. They had not spoken on the drive to the hospital, each in their own world of fear and thoughts. I had turned to them in the car to reassure them and squeeze their hands. Now they were left with him and he was in a foul mood. I just had to get back to them.

I had been warned if I told the truth of what he had done, he would take the children away from me. I wouldn't see them again ... they would all be gone by the time I got home. Maybe if I told the doctors the truth, they would call the authorities and they would then remove the children from me. I was a bad mother for allowing this to happen ... what sort of home did I live in? The fear of losing my children was eating me up, and also quietly strengthening my resolve to escape. I was so fearful of being exposed. I truly believed my children would be taken away, so I lied and continued to tell my stupid made-up stories.

I was alone; the end result had been achieved.

Control. Isolation. Shame. Self-loathing.

He knew I was trying to get away, to escape. I just didn't know how. I had tried to get away on so many occasions and yet I was often thwarted; he seemed to have this sixth sense. My paranoia grew. How did he know what I was planning, what I was thinking? He watched me slowly, purposefully. I was acutely aware of my body language, facial expressions. These were all clues to him. I learnt to be emotionless. As added insurance to hinder any planned escape, he would always keep one child with him, even if I went to the supermarket. He knew I would not leave without all three children. He would time my shopping trips, so he would know if I had strayed to try and visit my family. He watched constantly, stalking around me in case I did something different, changed my routine.

I recalled another particularly brutal beating where he rained down punches and then threw me against a wall. As he left the room he decided to push the wardrobe which fell on top of me. *'The strength of the devil.'* The words of my mother echoed in my mind from when she once had told me one of her life lesson stories. The devil indeed. I lay there motionless on the bedroom floor, gripping the thin grey worn carpet with my fingernails, distracted by the scratching sound it made. I smelt the old wood of the wardrobe. A faint smell of mothballs became my focus as I played dead and waited for my opportunity to run. He had at the time been entertaining his current lady friend and he believed I wasn't behaving suitably towards her. My apparent rude, unsociable behaviour was the catalyst for the beating that ended with the wardrobe incident.

As I lay on the bedroom floor dazed and in pain, I began twitching my arms and feet to see if they were working. Whilst he was distracted I managed to quietly move my body and manoeuver the wardrobe to allow me room to move my limbs. It is sometimes strange how you feel no pain whilst you are in the moment – adrenaline or fear just makes you do things you think impossible. You do not feel.

I quickly made my way to his bedroom drawer and grabbed a handful of his money, his drugs and pills, threw it in a shoulder bag and just ran. I could not grab the children, I had no time. I just kept running.

I ran for my life. I was so scared, I just ran.

I made the mistake of looking back. I saw Jasmine's troubled face as she watched me scampering away, darting between trees. Her little face was pressed against the window as she waved to me. Returning the wave, I was inwardly fighting the urge to turn back to her. The children should not be witnessing this, living like this. I had to harden my heart.

The grand plan in this moment was to go somewhere and kill myself, to give up. The children would be better off without me. They would not have to listen to the anger and hear my tears, they would not have to feel this fear if I was no longer around. I could not go on any longer. I will kill myself before he killed me.

I moved along the footpath keeping close to the boundary fences, occasionally turning my head to see if he was behind me. At the sound of each approaching car I would brace my body – was it him? Eventually I stumbled upon a bus stop and with relief sat down on its hard wooden seats, waiting nervously to catch a bus into the nearest town. I didn't care what I looked like anymore. As the bus finally approached, I fossicked in my bag for some change and, ignoring the looks from the driver and other passengers, I climbed aboard and slumped my body against the window. When I reached the nearest city, I made my way off the bus and just continued walking. My body was beginning to ache; the adrenaline was wearing off. I was in pain. I looked like I felt and I felt like I had lost everything.

I kept my head down, looking at the dull grey pavement, walking the walk of the invisible. I walked aimlessly for a few kilometres until my tired body was relieved to see a hotel. Entering the red brick entrance, ignoring the guests in the dining area I booked myself a room for the night. I paid cash with his money and trudged up the stairs to the room. I had no hand luggage, no suitcase.

Locking the door behind me all I knew was that I wanted to be alone and die, but did not know what to do or how to do it. How do you end your life?

The weather was overcast and dreary, fitting my mood. I had nothing left. The blandness of the room fueled my despair. I lay on the bed and stared blankly out of the first-floor window at the patterns of the red brick outside. As my agitation grew I sat up to look out of the other window, watching as other people's lives went by, cars drove by. Where were they going? What were they doing? What lives do they have? They are living. My mind was scrambled with ridiculous thoughts, but then I stopped and looked, something familiar catching my attention.

Kmart. I can see Kmart. I smiled to myself.

Could I do it? Could I be so bold, so reckless? I walked to my shoulder bag, which I had flung on the bed, and looked at the wad of notes I had taken. I began to slowly count them – there was over $400.

If I spent his money I would get one hell of a beating. I was tired of caring. I had received a beating for no reason at all anyway, so I decided to spend it. I needed a new plan.

Walking over to Kmart, scanning the aisles I purchased a carry bag, some underwear, a dress, some pants, a top and some toiletries. Taking my new purchases back to the bleak hotel room, I then phoned the Greyhound bus and booked a one-way ticket to Adelaide.

This was my plan. I was going to disappear somewhere to kill myself and die quietly.

I never did have the courage to kill myself. Once there, all I could think of, while I sat in this dingy dirty Adelaide hotel room, was my children. I could see their faces. I would imagine how frightened they would be without me, how unprotected they would be without me. I missed them so much I ached to see them. I had to think of how to make a better life with them. I had to plan a life for them. I had to get away from him with them.

I was running out of his money and had to go back, face what was coming. I had been away for over a week. I needed to see my children. I rang the Greyhound bus and booked a one-way ticket back.

I'm sorry for leaving you, kids. I'm coming home. I'm so sorry.

9

HOW TO KILL A HUSBAND

If I wasn't brave enough to kill myself, maybe the next best option would be to kill him. Maybe that would be the only way I could break free, be safe, and live a quiet life. *And so this is who I am. What I have become?* He had reduced me to this. My favourite past time was now planning his murder. These wonderful daydreams of evil intent kept my spirits up and gave me a focus.

The idea had come to me quite simply ... the fallout from the usual Sunday roast. As part of the 'rules' each Sunday one must have a full roast; including lamb, potatoes, pumpkin, assorted vegetables and, of course, gravy. No lumps, but smooth and rich, not made from the packet but the juices of the meat. The roast was required to be served at approximately 12:30pm – no later. After all, these are the rules.

As the roast was cooking away and the beautiful odours filled the kitchen, I decided to fill the salt and pepper containers. For them to be empty would be a failing on my part, so I absent-mindedly started this mundane task. He had called into the kitchen several times, checking out that I was following instructions, arranging the plates, checking the heat in the oven and the texture of the gravy. I could smell his beer breath against my neck each time he walked by, and I knew his eyes were on me without turning around.

It was approaching 12:20pm and, from experience, I was meticulous with my timing. The roast was cooked to perfection, the vegetables perfectly crisp with the corners caramelised. I began to serve it up on the plates, just heated. (You do not serve a roast on an unheated plate; more rules).

As the delicious feast was served he went to add the salt. One small mistake was about to ruin my day as the salt tumbled out of the container all over his beloved, meticulously cooked roast. Why had I not checked the lid was on tighter? The redness leeching up his neck and the black pinpoints of his narrowed eyes warned me that this was not a laughing matter. In an instant, his plate and the roast dinner went flying past my head, followed closely by my own plate. With screaming white anger and mindless abuse, he concluded that it was my attempt to poison him. I was planning to kill him off, with salt?

Then the thought struck me: I *could* poison him, kill him. If I was going to really kill him, what would I do?

As I sat there shielding myself from his blows and nursing my broken body, my secret thoughts gave me solace, a purpose. I devised my grand murderous plan, a heroin overdose. The plan was to drug him with sleeping pills or Rohypnol and wait for him to fall unconscious. Certain he was completely out cold, I would then inject him with an overdose of heroin or hot shot, call it what you will.

It was a great idea. The only thing that concerned me was, what if he woke up? It was well known that he had a fear of needles – how would I find a vein, where would I get the heroin? Maybe this idea wasn't as foolproof or straight forward as I thought. There must be another way.

***

In the early evening after the ill-fated roast dinner, I cleaned the mess from the walls and finished off the dishes. The fantasies and scenarios I played out in my mind were a welcome distraction and a source of constant amusement in those dark times.

As I stared into the kitchen sink, I gently drew patterns with the bubbles that remained from the washing up. I caressed them into the centre of the sink, turned the tap on and let the water trickle slowly, washing the bubbles down the plughole. We don't leave bubbles in the sink – another stupid rule.

I admired my clean sink and sighed. *I need to get away.*

10

THE BEGINNING OF THE PLAN

I fear quite a few things in life. Despite the usual fears of heights, spiders and mice, though, my fears are more of danger, of fear itself. I also fear being alone, and fear taking a shower when no one else is in the house. It took years to train myself with neurotic routines to ensure I was safe on those days when I found myself alone. I am scared of walking alone especially in the dark, always jumping at shadows, expecting someone to jump out and get me.

I was always on edge, always jumpy. He seemed to think it was hysterically funny to hide from me within the house. He would jump out of nowhere to scare me, then get close to my face and whisper quietly, 'Not yet.' I would often get a punch or two aimed at my body for good measure. This was a source of great amusement for him, but it did little to help my frayed nerves.

As a family we had lived in our new home in Anglesea for only a month before I fled. After many failed attempts, the final plan and process to leave had been hatched a year earlier just after the incident with the smashed bottle. He had decided we'd sell everything we owned and move three and half thousand miles away to Western Australia as a family. His plan was that he would fly over and I would dutifully follow with the three children after tying up all the loose ends. I had agreed it was an excellent idea and went along with his grand plan, all the while thinking there was no way I intended to follow him. My mind ticked over with all the possibilities of planning my final escape. I would just take the children and disappear, hide away where he would never find me, reinvent myself, change our names and identities. I was so thrilled with this option of escape, however I kept my emotions in check so not to give myself away.

Just prior to our move to Western Australia.

At the last minute he changed plans. With the finesse of a magician performing his grand finale, he waved some tickets in my face, showing me that he would travel over with Jasmine and Matthew, leaving me and our youngest child Devon behind. His intention was for me to sell the remaining furniture and pack up the rest of the house. Two weeks later when I had tied up all the loose ends, I would join him. He had ensured that by taking the two eldest children, I would be guaranteed to follow.

To say I was devastated was an understatement. My face said it all, I couldn't hide my dismay. I didn't have time to put on my mask. A tsunami of colour drained from my face, and the hole in my stomach from an invisible punch crushed my organs, making it difficult to breathe. He must have read my mind. He looked at me and smiled. He knew it, he had played his trump card.

He then proceeded to sell off all our possessions. Gathering funds for his trip, he sold off the kids' toys and bikes, and my beloved vintage furniture pieces and trinkets. All of it gone.

He had also arranged that we would be staying with his parents.

It was all sorted out. I fleetingly remembered my wedding. It seemed my life had been this way for a long time. I just had to follow the prompts. I had no escape. I felt the crushing weight of defeat.

As the day came for him to leave with the children, my heart sank. I was empty, lost and consumed with worry. Would they be comforted? Would they be cared for, would they miss me? Would he fill their little heads with lies and twisted stories?

I hugged them close for as long as I could. I kissed their little faces and tears rolled down my cheeks. Then he was gone. He knew I would not abandon them, he knew that. He knew I would follow.

He also knew I was pulling away, getting stronger. He knew or sensed that I was looking for escape routes, and for once his paranoia was justified. I spent most of my waking moments planning how to escape. He intensified his efforts to thwart my plans and stifle my opportunities. He was always observing, always controlling. Always watching. There was no freedom, no respite. The move west to isolation was his way of limiting my opportunities.

As I write this now it does sound rather unbelievable, and I still wonder and feel the guilt of why I did not just go. Why I did not just call the police? The reality was I was constantly afraid of a beating, so afraid he would kill me. If I was dead the kids would be left with him. These thoughts make no sense now, but at the time, in my weakened mental state, it did.

I had no friends of my own, and had been alienated from my family. They thought I was weak, pathetic, a fool. *'Just leave him. It's easy,'* they would say. *'You don't have to put up with that.'* I could hear their words ringing in my head, see the derision on their faces. If only it was that simple.

My isolation, my loneliness and my fragile mind, not to mention my financial dependence, played into his hands. He left for Perth, and two weeks later I boarded the plane as organised with a heavy heart, a crying 18-month-old and a battered suitcase.

I arrived at Perth Airport to see him watching intently as I came off the plane. He was looking for clues, to what I'm not sure.

'Thank fuck you're here. So who were you sleeping with while I was away?' he asked, then began his rant about his parents and how naughty the kids were.

The cold steel of a rabbit trap snapped itself shut around my heart, around my life. *That's it. I'm trapped, forever trapped.*

We arrived at his parents' house, a grey brick Spanish-type villa. The children ran out and threw themselves at me, each clamouring for attention. I held them close and kissed their faces, necks and warm little hands. I breathed them in and squeezed them tight. His parents also seemed pleased, or was that relieved, to see me. They had prepared me a meal.

He showed me around the house and where we would be sleeping. Relieved to put down my luggage, I sat on the bed as the tears just flowed. I couldn't stop them. Alone in my sadness, no family. Just them.

He hissed at me to get it together in front of his parents, to stop making a fool of him. As much as I tried I just couldn't stop the flow of tears. My head was pounding with the effort of trying to stop the floodgates, and I begged to just be left to be. Jasmine wrapped her arms around me, hugging me tight. Matthew nestled in close to my chest and I held him tight. This made the tears worse. By now, Jasmine had taken on the role of comforter to me and patted me like one would a small child. More tears flowed. This was now my life.

For a few weeks things went along as before. He would make attempts to work and get a job; he would argue with his parents, he would argue with me. He would continually drink. Eventually his parents had had enough and wanted us to leave, handing over some money to help us get a rental property. Within the week we ended up getting our own house, and with more privacy he returned to his usual form.

It was during this time in our new home that he went out on one of his escapades to who knows where. Little did I care, to be honest. I decided to venture out on a walk with the children. It would be wise to get my bearings, make note of any emergency phone numbers and escape routes. This sounds strange, but I was always doing this as it gave me a strange comfort. After a nice morning walking around the neighbourhood and playing in a park with the children, we returned home happy and exhausted.

I was musing that I had not heard birds singing. I missed the sound of magpies and their morning song. In Western Australia, birds did not sing the way they did in Victoria. This was something that intrigued me, and I was wondering why when I heard a loud bang rom the bedroom.

I had not realised that he was home until I went to the bedroom and saw he was laying under a huge mirror. There was a large hole in the wall and he seemed quite vague. Having no idea what had happened, I warily took in the scene. Not wanting or able to move the heavy mirror or get closer, I wasn't sure what he was doing or what had happened. He lay there awhile and seemed to regain consciousness. Opening his eyes, his pinpoint focus was on me and he was furious. I had done this to him. I had tried to kill him.

Still trying to understand what had happened, I was not quick enough to make a move as the quicksand of fear kept me transfixed. With devil strength he pushed the mirror away and leapt up. As he did so, he smashed my head into the wall. I fell back in pain and surprise onto the bedroom floor. He continued to kick me several times in the back and stomach. I curled up in a ball trying to protect myself, to deflect the blows and silence my cries of pain. As the blood rushed through my ears like crashing waterfalls, I could vaguely hear the children's frightened crying. Hopeful they would stay away and not see this brutality. He gave me one final hell of a back hander across the face. I could taste and feel the sweet thickness of blood. He then walked away, but not before a backward glance.

'I've got a bloody bump on my head from you, ya bitch. That'll teach you.' With that he went to the kitchen, got himself a beer and sat himself down in his favourite chair.

Staring at the red lines on the dark blue carpet, I lay there unable to move, huddled in pain and confusion. *What just happened? I don't know what just happened?* I gingerly attempted to stand up, rolling onto my knees and using my arms for support. With each inward breath the stabbing pain pinched my ribs. My lower back ached and would not click into place or allow me to stand straight. The tops of my thighs and legs were feeling the effects from where his boots had kicked into them. My head was pounding as the blood rushed and expanded into my hair follicles. Every sense was alert, pulsating with electric shocks of pain.

These beatings were intensifying as he continued to lose control. *I must get away, I have to.*

Returning to the kitchen I went about my domestic chores, focusing on what I could control. I set about regaining my order, not speaking, not making eye contact, not wishing to raise his ire, just wishing to be invisible. I methodically prepared the kids some tea, praying he would just fall asleep in a drunken stupor and die. He did fall asleep, but that was it.

I quietly steeled my resolve. *I am going to escape, I will get away. I know no one here but I am going.* I had no funds to go back home so I had to find another way. My family were not in a financial position to help, nor was our relationship good. I had disappointed them again by following him here.

'Get the police to bring the children back,' my family had said, but it was not that easy. I had no orders out for custody, and he could always lie better than I told the truth. He would tell people that I gave my kids up as I was a slut mother, a druggie, a bad mother. I was terrified people would believe him. Silly, really. I know now, but then I didn't.

The next morning, he went out again on one of his mystery trips. He was confident now that he could leave all the kids with me as I knew no-one, had no money, no car or even knew where I was.

I rustled through his drawers and found some money he had stashed away. I then dressed the kids and made my way with them to one of the bus stops I had seen on my daily walks, then caught a bus into the nearest city. Vanity no longer mattered to me as I limped and hobbled along the road, three raggle taggle children following behind. Having no real idea of what I was doing, I found the Department of Social Security office and asked to see someone. The person behind the counter allotted me a number. Anxiety and nausea fought for control of my stomach as I waited to see a social worker. I was so embarrassed and ashamed as the words fell from my lips, telling them what had bought me here, what had happened. I pleaded with them to help me.

The woman took a good look at me, glancing at the children and said rather grandly that she could assist me. My face flooded with crimson … I felt so small. I would be relocated to a woman's refuge. She handed me some emergency funds from her desk drawer and sent me in a taxi on my way. I had no idea where I was going or what lay ahead, but I was past caring, and the children were tired and hungry. I hadn't packed extra clothes or food; in fact, I had nothing much on me, only my purse and ID. I hadn't even packed a suitcase.

The taxi pulled up outside an old house and I was ushered inside to speak to the manager or person in charge. I was shown a room, given a key, told the rules about drinking, drugs and men, and shown where the communal kitchen was.

I was also introduced to the other women. I was the only white woman there.

The women seemed very interested and curious about us, and seemed particularly enchanted by my young daughter with her blue eyes, blonde hair and cute baby ways. The women and assorted children were happy to entertain and play with my kids whilst I just sat, lost in my own world. I had no idea what I was doing. The women prepared a communal meal and I gratefully accepted. I could barely speak I was so defeated, so I just smiled at them and nodded my head in thanks.

The beauty of children is they make friends easily and enjoy an adventure, and to them this was indeed a great adventure. For a fleeting moment the children made me smile – they were so adaptable, laughing and playing with their new friends.

I needed sleep and, before long, I excused us all and went to our rooms. The manager found us some clothes and nightwear, then the day was finally done. I briefly thought of his anger when he knew we were gone, but at this point I didn't care anymore. I had to make new plans.

I stayed in this place for three weeks. To this day I have no idea where it was. It was strange and yet peaceful, a ramshackle old house with basic facilities. I was left alone, just free to be. Emotionless, thoughtless, I walked around like a haunted soul. The children just played and ran around wild and silly with the other children. Wearing nothing but underwear, they laughed and played in the heat. The kids turned a most beautiful honey brown in the sun, their hair became sun-kissed blonde. They were so happy and carefree, and had not once asked about their dad.

Eventually, though, the time came to decide what to do. I couldn't stay there forever, as much as I'm sure the children would have liked to. I wanted to get home to Victoria. On the small pension I was receiving, it would take me years.

I then steeled myself for the call I was going to make, and the beginning of the final plan. I didn't care what I had to endure, I was going home and there was only one way to do it.

I called him.

11

A STRANGE KIND OF LUCK

The Australian bush can withstand all – fire, flood, and tempests. Trees stand strong and unbreakable, a gentle flutter of leaves or a force of winds. They stand with purpose and being.

As I sat under a native gum fidgeting with its harsh bark, I lay my head against its trunk, as if by some magical power of nature, I could hug the tree's strength into my soul. I gazed up to the bluest of skies, and a deep breath escaped from my lungs as I knew what I had to do. I arose from my silent tree, as a resolute calm guided me to the phone box standing alone at the end of the dirt road, its faded red handset and glass cubicle covered in faded graffiti. I had nothing to give, nothing to lose.

He answered the phone, sounding surprised to hear my voice. I focused on the swaying leaves as my nerve faltered.

'I will come back to you if you get me back to Victoria.' My words were short, sharp and to the point. 'We can start again.' I almost choked on my insincerity saying these words. As a distraction, I pulled faces at myself in the reflective glass of the phone box.

My plan consisted of getting back home to Victoria. This was all my grand idea was at this moment in time, and I needed him and his finances to get me there. Once I was in my home state I would leave him for good, however I could, whatever the price I had to pay.

He eagerly agreed that he would get us back to Victoria if I came home, saying how sorry he was, how he missed me and a thousand other platitudes that I had heard a hundred times before. They meant nothing.

I made arrangements to leave the refuge and thanked the women for their kindness. The kids said goodbyes to their friends and seemed to be quite OK going back to see their Dad. To the children, it was like we had a fun holiday. The women at the refuge must have thought I was quite strange, aimlessly walking around all day or just sitting quietly staring into space – a mute woman, with such wild, noisy, joyful children. I finally did speak to thank them for allowing me that quiet time and space. It was a strange time in an unknown place.

I packed a borrowed suitcase with our few belongings and wandered down a dusty road with three little children in tow. The children started to kick at the stones on the road. Their joy seemed to have left them as they realised we were going back to him. Devon held onto her brother's hand, her security when things troubled her. Jasmine's face was brooding and sullen – she knew what we were going back to. She dawdled last along the dusty road, in no hurry to get where we needed to be. I made up a happy story for the kids, telling them we were going back to Victoria. I reassured them it would be OK, but in my heart I knew it was a lie. I had arranged to meet him away from the refuge for security reasons, and from there he would take me back to the house from which we had fled weeks earlier.

I sensed him first, the hairs on my arms standing erect as they shimmied up my neck, the rush cooling my body in the stifling heat. In the distance he was walking towards me, striding confidently, the hunter retrieving its prey. Those familiar feelings of panic began to rise as my body betrayed my pretend bravery, goosebumps on my skin, bile in my throat, the knot twisting in my stomach choking my breath.

I gently closed my eyes, took an inward breath and with my head tilted back to the sky I said a silent prayer to some higher power to help me be strong and safe. *I have a plan. I am getting us home.* He eyed me warily, the hunter not quite sure his prey is slayed.

His focus changed to the children as tears welled in his eyes – he was happy and emotional to see them. Hugging them, he turned to me and under his breath muttered, 'Don't ever take them away from me again, or I'll fucking kill you.'

I let that slide and got in the car. No clues, no emotion.

The car drove along highways and streets. I still had no idea where I was or what part of Western Australia I was living in. I looked for clues as street signs flashed by. Finally as we turned into the driveway of the rental home. I gave myself a moment to remember why I left. Like the native gum I held my body in a strong stance, waiting for the storm, trying to bluff myself to have a strength I did not feel. I walked towards the front door.

Stepping inside, the house was spotless. Of course it would be. A bunch of native flowers were sitting on the kitchen table, with a card next to them waiting for me to open it. My heart was hardened, I didn't really care. He carried in my one small suitcase containing the collection of clothes I had been given for the kids. He casually placed the day's mail on the table. Sitting on his comfy couch, he drew the children into his arms and as he cuddled them, he began his usual subtle questioning of them. *Did we live in a nice house on our holiday? Where had we been? Did they make friends? Who had Mummy seen? Did Mummy make new friends?* The children told him of their days in the sun and their new friends, of all the games they had played, naive to his ulterior motives.

I went into the old kitchen, the drabness of the faded walls with its peeling paint and cracked lino feeding into my misery. I put the kettle on to make myself a coffee, rearranging coffee cups and everything on the kitchen bench. These simple tasks restored my order. I felt alien in this house, an interloper; I didn't belong.

The children finally extracted themselves from his arms and kisses, running with glee to their rooms, familiarising themselves with their toys, their life. My heart weighed heavy for my children. They didn't deserve this lifestyle. Coming and going, running and returning, waiting for the next chapter of chaos. Was it too much to ask for – a settled life, love and security, not all this moving and running away, this constant upheaval? Overwhelmed with guilt and regret, I sought order to stop myself from drowning. As I turned, I saw him watching me from the kitchen door. He walked into the kitchen and with purpose rearranged the kitchen bench and the canisters how he liked them – all in order with labels to the front, same width apart. I sighed wearily and offered him a coffee to break the tension whilst he checked the mail.

Suddenly he broke into the biggest smile.

'Guess what Jan, guess what?' He seemed genuinely happy about something, yet I eyed him suspiciously. 'We have a commission house ready for us in Victoria if we can get back there.'

We had been on the waiting list for government public housing for a few years. I had put our name on the list many years earlier as we never seemed to stay anywhere longer than a year. He had usually argued or offended most of the neighbours, or started some strange war with them. I hated having to constantly move and resettle the children. I craved routine, especially as Jasmine had just started school. Children need stability, I needed order.

Bursts of long-lost colour exploded inside me. I saw this as a sign; in my search for hope this was a genuine sign. Something good was going to happen. I smiled back at him, and for the briefest moment as our eyes met, we were genuinely happy.

'I'll phone straight away and let them know we are interested. We can go back to Victoria.' Off he went to find a phone box to follow up this seemingly good fortune, a stroke of luck. As he walked out of the house I could barely contain my joy. Not only were we going back to Victoria, but we would get a house. I said a silent prayer of thanks to whoever had been listening.

He soon returned to tell me they would pay for our furniture to be transported back as a relocation. We had limited furniture at this point, having sold all my favourite pieces when we moved here. I had no real emotional attachment to this house, these things. We were informed we would need to live in a caravan park for a few weeks until the house was finished being built. All we had to do was book a bus trip back. I actually hugged him, I was so thrilled.

Within three weeks we were travelling on a Greyhound bus heading across the Nullarbor. I again packed a suitcase, and all the belongings we had taken with us to Western Australia, to finally return to Victoria. This new move was to a place called Anglesea, which was nestled away on the Surf Coast of Victoria.

All I knew of Anglesea was from a family day trip we had taken there in Dad's Volkswagen when I was little. The memory of that trip made me smile. As usual I had carried on and sooked like a spoilt brat to sit in the very back compartment. This was the prized position to have amongst us kids. The winding roads had made me incredibly carsick and I was not well. We stopped near the Anglesea River for a picnic lunch, which I could not enjoy. Dad could not drive any further on our day trip due to my vomiting in the car. I had ruined everyone's day.

The other thing I knew was that Anglesea had just been devastated by the Ash Wednesday bushfires and was in the midst of rebuilding.

The bus trip home across the Nullabor was over three and half thousand kilometres, a shocker. Having injured my back, I was in pain from a recent beating and it hurt to sit on a comfy couch, let alone a bus seat. He decided he needed a whole seat to himself. Stoned off his head and dosed up on sleeping tablets, he promptly fell asleep. I, on the other hand, had three kids under six wriggling all over me, moaning, uncomfortable and just plain bored.

After two days I was in so much pain and desperately needed to move my cramped body. Thankfully the bus pulled over at the Great Australian Bite to do the tourist thing, and everyone could stretch their legs and admire the view. Herding the children in front of me, I managed to finally get out of the bus, hunched in half, unable to stand straight and in shocking pain. I am ashamed to say I held a very impressive two-year-old tantrum, shouting obscenities, spitting and raging from pain. I cried and screamed whilst refusing to get back on the bus. I was embarrassing him so much that he finally agreed to take the kids for a while, so I could stretch out. I sullenly agreed and was finally coaxed back onto the bus by the driver, ignoring the looks of our fellow travelers.

Finally, after four long days on the bus, we made it back to Melbourne. From there we took another coach to Anglesea, having booked ourselves into a caravan park for the next few weeks while we waited for the house to be finished. Our limited furniture and belongings arrived a few days later by truck.

As we settled into caravan park life, we got to choose and look at the houses on offer. He liked a house in Aireys Inlet, a small township outside of Anglesea. He wanted us all to live there, however to me it was isolated. As I didn't have a car and would need to walk everywhere, it was a good few miles to the school and shops. I didn't want to fall into the trap of isolation again.

In saying that, though, I would have taken it if I had not set eyes on Ramsay St. Another of the houses on offer was in Anglesea itself, and we walked over to look at it. From the very second, I saw it, even half built, I knew. *This was my home.*

I glanced across the heathland, I heard the sea crash against the cliffs, I smelt the fresh sea air – and everything in my being told me I was home. That feeling to this day has never left me when I return and stand on those cliffs. This was my home, and nothing and no one would take it away from me. Ever.

This was my reward, my redemption.

'This is it,' I said to him.

'No, I don't like it,' he replied as he walked away, waving his hand in dismissal.

'No, this is it. It is perfect – the kids can play amongst the bush and the beach is close by. This is perfect.'

I would not give in on this and, like the native gums that surrounded the bushland of this home, I was strong. I stood still.

We faced off across the floor of an unbuilt house, then strangely and quietly he agreed. We caught a bus into the city to sign the required paperwork and await the house being completed. It was at this time a concrete floor plan, an empty shell of wooden frames, but I could see where the bedrooms and the porch would be.

I could see it all in my mind's eye.

Unfortunately, it took longer than a few weeks to finish the build, and we spent six long winter months in a caravan park where he went absolutely stir crazy, a one-man tyrant. I would head off to the camp laundry to wash the clothes and bath the children, but mainly to escape his nonstop tirades on life and his vitriol on my neediness to live here in this god forsaken town. I remained unmoved. His most pressing concern during our stay seemed to be his inability to get all the TV channels he wanted to watch his shows on. He would stalk the caravan park to see who had what channels and was furious that his viewing seemed to be limited. It only took a few days till he had worked out a solution – he cut everyone else's TV antennas in the caravan park. He then had clear TV reception. The problem was solved for him, but it did not make us tenant of the year.

I cringed with embarrassment as I scurried like a furtive rat between the vans, hoping no-one would see me to take me to task and ask me to speak to him. He argued with absolutely everyone he made eye contact with – the park cleaners, the postman, the old people who used to sit outside to feed the birds, visitors to the park, anyone who drove fast or slow through the park; no one was safe from his abuse.

After a while he found new drinking mates, new women to party with and in general continued to be a right arsehole. On the positive, these new friends took him out of the park for a few hours, so we could all have some respite. I knew his intention was for me to wilt under the embarrassment and shame of his behaviour, and therefore agree to his preferred solution of where to live, but this time I dug my heels in, I didn't care what people thought of me anymore. I was completely desensitised to him now. No matter how he tried to get me to react, I wouldn't. No matter what he handed out, I would take it. I was getting a house, I would finally find stability for the children. Jasmine had just started school and next year Matthew would be at kinder. They would have a security and build friendships, play sport, be part of a community.

It was in the late spring of 1983 that the house was eventually finished, and the day came when we could finally move in. I had spent many a winter's day walking up the hill to watch the progress of the house build with the children. When the builders were gone, we would sneak in and walk around, imagining where our rooms would be as we carefully balanced over the wooden frames. We would sit swinging our legs on the floor beams, spending hours talking about what we would do when we lived there, what we would buy, what colours we would have in our rooms. Our dreams were so simple and carefree.

As I stood in front of the house, my home, I breathed in the joy and hope of the spring day. The breeze gave a hint of lazy summer days to come, the air perfumed with scents of life. It was the type of day where you could believe that life could be perfect, and so it was on this day when we were finally given the keys to our freshly painted new house. If I was allowed to show emotion I would have cried tears of happiness, but I held all my glee swirling around like fluffy pink fairy floss inside me. I have never in my life felt so blessed and at home. I had found my bubble. What strange kind of luck had bought me here; it had done so for a reason? I started to believe I would be OK. How wrong had I been?

Fast forward to three months later as I lay on the lounge room floor, questioning my decision to come back, remembering all the moments that had led me to now. The spectre of him still loomed large; he was not going to give up that easily. I knew the lighting of the fire was just the beginning.

I had come home, but what would it cost me?

12

COMING HOME

PART 2

The night we had arrived home from the refuge, to a home devoid of furniture and belongings, we slept on the lounge room floor. Our beds were made from some blankets which had been left behind – to my amusement, he had forgotten to look in the linen cupboard. I wasn't foolish enough to think it was a small act of kindness on his part. The children created a super cosy cubby as we all snuggled together, playing our dreaming game. What did we need to buy for our new home? What would we do in our new home? How could we do up our bedrooms, what would we need? Sleep was difficult to come by as the children chattered excitedly of all the things we could go shopping for and how exciting it would be. I played along with them, although my thoughts were more along the lines of how I was going to afford to start again.

Eventually the kids fell asleep. Thankful for the slivers of moonlight through the lounge room window, I extracted myself from their clinging arms and silently made my way to the kitchen. The trees cast a scary shadow as they swayed in the darkness against the kitchen windows and I wondered if he was out there, watching me. Each small noise startled me into awareness as I sat on the cold of the kitchen floor. Twisting and turning to new sounds, the crack of a tree branch, the rustle of leaves – was that a knock at the window? Everything seemed overly exaggerated in my heightened state, as it so often does when the night comes. I was wide awake and jumping at shadows.

As the children slept on their makeshift bed, I started to plan. I needed to work out a budget and a list. I scrummaged around in my handbag, finding my notebook and pen, having to hold them close to my face to see what I was writing in the darkness. The calming process of making that list gave me a sense of control and order. I just wish I had something to make a coffee.

Priority number one, apart from getting light and power, was beds for the kids. I could put what clothes and few possessions we had into cardboard boxes till I could afford drawers. We really needed a lounge suite – the floor was going to get very uncomfortable – and of course a TV. Whilst a TV may not have seemed like a necessity, it was important to me to have some normality in our lives and I needed to have their routine back. If Jasmine missed much more of the TV show *Neighbours*, she would have a meltdown. Routine and order, I craved this simple lifestyle.

Needing to find some cheap second-hand furniture stores, I thought I would ask Paula to take me into town to get the basics. Paula was a great bargain hunter and seemed to know where to get stuff. She also had her own car, which was a big help. It had been a relief to see Paula again – she had come straight around the morning after our return, notified by the kids that we were back. Much to my surprise, Paula came bearing gifts. Paula had purchased the kids' bikes and a few of their toys off him, knowing that the kids would be upset to lose them and unable to bare the fact he was just going to throw them in the tip. For this gesture of kindness, I would be eternally grateful. Although I offered her money, she refused.

Paula and I then planned our shopping trip to get some of the things I would need when my government pension next came through in a fortnight's time. In the meantime, Paula rustled up a few things she had at home to help us get by – a kettle and some cups so we could at least have coffee, a few pots and pans to cook with, cutlery, crockery to eat on, a foam mattress to share, and more bedding. We set up camp in the lounge room, eating our meals on the floor, sleeping on the floor and resting our backs against the walls as the sun streamed through the windows. The children spent most of their waking hours playing outside as I had not as yet settled them back into school and kinder. I didn't want our living conditions to be known, as I was fearful of losing the children to child protection.

It seemed a long two weeks till our long-awaited shopping day finally arrived. We left all the children with Paula's husband and headed into town to hunt up some furniture bargains. Knowing this would just about leave me broke for the rest of the fortnight, my priority was getting the kids' beds. After some great haggling from Paula, I managed to buy a bed each for the kids and a two-seater couch which was a bonus. I ignored the horrendous swirly maroon and gold pattern – it was a comfy couch, and I could save for something better when finances improved. I saw a beautiful set of drawers that was a bargain for $36 and I put them on layby. I had 4 weeks to pay them off.

We squashed the beds and couch into Paula's van, and we doubled ourselves in half from the cramped conditions of trying to fit it all in. As we drove home wedged between furniture, with tall tales and laughter we happened across another stroke of good fortune, spotting a half-broken TV aerial on the side of the road. Paula pulled the van over and we quickly ran into the paddock, scavenging the aerial to add to our hodge podge collection. Pushing the disjointed pieces into the back of the van, we roared with laughter as this simple task provided us so much delight and amusement. We had struck gold.

We decided from this incredible find that it was a sign, so our next stop should be one of those dodgy hire purchase places that let you rent and then buy electrical items. I proudly purchased a TV and video recorder in some shonky deal, making arrangements to have the funds taken out of my fortnightly pension. At the time I was not thinking or even considering the ridiculous amount of interest I would be paying. This was the first real new thing I had ever owned.

I was so proud and could not wait to get home to show the kids what we had. We were rich. We had a new TV and video recorder. The excitement and joy on the kids' faces was worth every bit of the triple interest I would be paying. They were beside themselves with their 'new beds' and our 'new' couch. Paula's husband set up our TV aerial – we had TV.

Finally, we had some normal.

When the theme song to *Neighbours* came on that night and we all sat back to watch on our very squashy couch, it was like we had won the lottery. Could life get any better?

13

THE GAME

PART 2

He decided he would call by unannounced every other day – yelling abuse, disrupting our lives and constantly making threats. He would seem to just appear at the doorstep or from behind a fence or tree. I would never know when.

Self-preservation and vigilance became a part of our daily routine, always needing to have the doors and windows locked. I had purchased some thick curtains that hung off some wooden dowel. These were closed shut each night, no gaps to spy in – although some nights I felt he was watching me, so I would place pegs along the closings to secure them tight and then sit myself away from view, hiding in darkness when the children were in bed. Before we settled in for the night I would scour the garden, ensuring nothing that could be used as a missile was left outside, an errant cricket bat, a bike or shoes. When I walked the children to school and kinder I would always be checking to make sure he wasn't hiding in the bushland, listening for the telltale sound of footsteps on gravel or a broken twig, birds taking flight. I would keep the children close within the property boundaries so we could run inside to safety if we needed. I felt safer when they were an arm's distance away. Feelings of dread and fear would swallow me up when they ventured to play with friends or darted down the back tracks on their bikes. The sound of a far-off siren would immediately make me think something had happened to them. A constant electric shock of fear and foreboding ran through my body, its power draining.

I would never know when or how he would arrive – he just appeared. My body became a good antenna; I continued to sense his presence. He face would appear at the window or he would knock at the door.

Sometimes he would just sit and watch me, and I'd watch him from behind the safety of my closed curtains. After calling the police, they would take their time to turn up. He would just disappear into thin air before they arrived, laughing at me and pointing to where he would be hiding in the bush. I would ask the police to go look for him, my voice urgent at times and possibly hysterical. They just thought I was crazy, paranoid.

This was the way it was, our new pattern of living. Once again, we adapted to our new normal.

At the start of May 1984, as autumn leaves were falling and the season was coming to an end, I had a small flicker of hope that things had changed. He had not called around for over two weeks, and whilst I was hopeful he had stopped his games, his quietness gave me a sense of unease.

Meandering up the hill holding Devon's soft warm little hand, we were returning from our daily walk of taking the older children to their respective schools. Devon loved to chatter away, her childish conversations and antics a source of amusement and distraction. I loved this time with her, this routine. It was a walk of a few kilometres there and back and we were always happy to finally reach home at the top of the hill. After such a long walk Devon would curl up on her bed and have a morning nap, with hands stuffed full of her dummies. In a form of domestic contentment I went about my daily chores. I was so contented that I had become distracted, let my guard down – and had forgotten to lock the doors.

Swinging the washing basket on my hip with the familiarity of carrying a child, I made my way outside to the clothes line. The clothes jumbled and danced as the basket fell, making the lightest of sounds as it hit the concrete path. He stood in front of me, soundless, motionless. I wasn't quick enough or alert enough to see it coming, but I felt the blow. Falling sideways, as the smell of clean washing filled my nostrils, I held my face, my mind dazed and confused. Startled back to reality, I felt fear as his shoes kicked into me. All those feelings I had prayed I would never feel again came rushing back to me, crushing my organs till I could breathe no more. The blackness of pain came like molten lava oozing under my skin and flooding into my brain. I felt a quiet agony – weak and scared.

As autumn leaves floated from the trees and my clean washing sat amidst the remnants of crushed leaves and soil, the wattle bird whistled from high in the tree, drowning out his words. *What was he saying?* I didn't understand. My head was ringing – or was that buzzing, what was that sound? I tried desperately to make sense of his words, holding my head to keep the sounds still.

He looked at me and smiled. 'So, you get it now? You want me to come back home to keep you safe?'

I nodded, afraid and confused. He reached down to grab my arm to help me to my feet. Holding me close to him, he gently placed his arm around my back to guide me inside.

What had I just agreed to? *No, no. You mustn't come in, you mustn't.* Holding my body stiff, I tried to speak but the words were stuck, a furball of fear in my throat. I could see the phone through the kitchen window and he turned to see what had caught my gaze.

'Go on, ring the coppers, ring your friends.' His grip tightened.

I lowered my eyes and tried to think it through. *Think Jan, think.* He moved to stand in front of me, gripping my chin, forcing me to look into his eyes. He ran the back of his hand along my face. I froze.

'Please be quiet. Devon is asleep, please don't scare her,' I implored.

The children were just beginning to settle and feel safe. I didn't want him to frighten her, I didn't want to have to nurse them through their fears and anxieties again.

'Scare her? She's my fucking kid!' he screamed in my face.

I had said the wrong thing. Like a long dormant volcano, his anger erupted. The veins on his neck bulged blue, his eyes became dark and frightening. He walked me further inside, again gripping my arms with his bony hands. I felt them digging into me. He walked me into the lounge room and, as he pushed me away, he sat on my maroon and gold couch. I let him sit there, I sat on the floor.

Time went so slowly. The tick of the clock seemed so loud.

I watched the clock, and he watched me.

'I have to get Matthew from kinder,' I said in a small voice.

'OK, go. I'll stay here with Devon.' It was back to this old game. He saw the distress on my face and smiled. I could do nothing.

I felt sick, him being in my home. It was my sacred space. A thousand spiders seemed to crawl under my skin as he began to walk around and look at what I had. He touched my things, looked at my lists, my mail, then he would look back at me. He was memorising it all.

When the clock struck 1:30 it was time to collect Matthew. I pretended I needed to get my cardigan from the bedroom, taking the chance to grab a few loose coins, squeezing them tight so they would not make a sound. I quietly placed my hand in my pocket.

'I'll be back as soon as I can,' I whispered in a small voice.

Fighting a wave of nausea about to drown me, I left him in my home. This was my sanctuary, my safety. These were my things. I silently prayed he would not wreck anything. I had to get him out of there. I wasn't doing this again, he wasn't staying. He would never leave.

As I walked down the hill towards the shops, I knew there was a phone box on the corner. I called the police. I also rang Paula and asked her to collect Matthew. Explaining what had happened, I asked that she keep Matthew with her. She also offered to collect Jasmine from school later in the day, and keep the kids safe at her place.

Walking back up the hill to my house, a hundred heartbeats echoed in my ears, reverberating through my body. For a quiet moment, hiding behind a tree I observed him, a prize fighter sizing up their opponent. He was idly sitting on the verandah having a smoke. His body was languid, relaxed, his legs were stretched out and crossed at the heels, not a care in his world.

He quickly sat upright and lent forward when he saw me. He eyed me suspiciously as I walked up the driveway. I walked up the steps with more calmness than I felt, and with a mad dash reached for the door. He managed to dive forward and, with the talons of an angry bird holding its prey, he latched on to my hand.

'What have you fucking done?' he hissed.

'I've called the police. You shouldn't be here. The courts say so.' I tried to sound brave, officious even, although I knew it was futile.

'Fuck the courts.' With that he let me go, and returned to sit idly on the porch.

I ran into the house locking the door behind me, and waited for the police to arrive. After what seemed an age the police car turned into the driveway. Upon disembarking from the car, the police approached him. I peered through the curtains and listened at the window like the neighbourhood gossip.

'G'day mate.' He pleasantly welcomed the police like he had not one care in the world.

'What are you doing here, mate? The lady doesn't want you here,' the police officer stated matter of factly. 'Causing a bit of trouble, are you?'

He raised his eyes at the policeman and giving a bit of a wink, his laugh confident. He boldly stated, 'The bloody missus calls me round cause she's feeling a bit lonely, wants me to hop into bed with her and then tells me to piss off. I don't get women these days. Dunno what they want. I'm happy to leave the ugly dragon here, mate. Just thought I'd stay here to let you know I'm not wanting to cause trouble.'

With that he got up from the porch, and with the policeman by his side he casually walked down my driveway, having a friendly chat with the policeman on the way out.

I stood at the window, a churning fury inside me at the reason he gave for being here, my annoyance growing with the ease in which this seemed to be resolved. I awaited the policeman's return, hoping he had at least charged him with breaking the restraining orders or, at best, scared him away.

The policeman returned and knocked on my door. I swung the door open, silently seething as he informed me, 'What a reasonable guy he seems to be. After all, he wouldn't have hung around for the police if he was going to cause trouble. Maybe it's just a misunderstanding.' Ignoring the red mark on my face, he said, 'Look Jan, he just wants to leave with no trouble. I suggest for you not to let him in the house next time.'

Did he really say those words to me? The blood curdled in my veins with white hot anger. But he didn't stop there.

'Blokes get a bit angry when women change their minds and kick them out.'

Standing there incredulous, I pointed to the mark on my face. I had not invited him in. *How dare he. This was not my fault. Fuck you.*

'I didn't let him in.' Sharp, angry words in rapid fire defense. I raised my voice. 'He snuck up on me, he hit me. I have court orders, he can't do that … he can't come near my house.' I continued to blurt out my indignation. Looking at his bland expression, I suspected the policeman believed the rumours were true. I was the crazy lady on the hill, the nutcase. My rantings were falling on deaf ears.

'Well, he's on his way now and you seem alright, so just let him move on,' came his response.

What was the point of the court orders or the police? I slammed the door hard in his face.

I'll give you fucking crazy.

14

GAME CHANGERS

For the first two years after I had left, the game was always the same. He would arrive, cause havoc, then disappear. The police would always just miss him as he hid in the bushland. This was his favourite part of the game, like grown-up hide and seek. He really thought he was some big-time criminal getting away with a crime, outsmarting the police and the system – which to be honest he was, as he was still getting away with it. He would often be hiding, watching them, and would turn up laughing and creating more havoc when they had left. I was becoming quite immune to it all, as at this point I understood it was just a stupid game. He thrived on my reaction, it kept me engaged with him in some sense. I made a conscious decision not to react.

However, the game was about to change again.

He then decided that he would ring the police station and make threats to kill me. The police would drive up to my house and request that I find a safe place to hide away as they could not protect me all the time. The police would then drive me several kilometres away to stay with a friend, keeping me away for an hour or two until they had a look around for him and deemed it safe for me and the children to return. This was a huge inconvenience and annoyance to me, when I believe the easier alternative would have been to arrest him. I believed that was what the restraining orders were for. Silly me.

This scenario played out a few times before I decided I had had enough, and once again had to engage a lawyer to make him stop. Next time the police came to ask me to leave, I refused to go and waited for whatever was going to come. This game then stopped.

Up until this point he had not really used the kids as a game tool, as he seemed more intent on disrupting my life. I was the target of his hatred. The mistake I made at the time was in engaging a lawyer, as it allowed him to open a new discussion about custody and visitation rights. He now requested he see the kids every other weekend, and that he would collect them from my home. I strongly opposed these orders as the kids would not be safe with him, and they were also frightened to go. Despite letters and supporting documents I had to the contrary to dispute his access rights, he put on a wonderful performance in court. He was granted weekend access from Friday night to Sunday afternoon.

As I sat in the cold greyness of the court, I was shocked and beyond distressed. How on earth was I to tell the kids this? They had their happy little routine going, they had friends and stability. I had been working so hard to get them to sleep at night, allay their fears and anxieties, to help them stop jumping at shadows. I had protected them from his anger and lifestyle as much as I could over the last few years, and now a court was introducing it all back to them.

He came to collect the children for his access weekend two weeks later, looking as smart and as confident as he felt. New jeans, smart shoes, face all shiny and clean – he looked like he had it all. He also came bearing gifts for each child. Despite me having a restraining order in place, he was still allowed to come and collect the kids at my home as I didn't have a car. He marched up the driveway like he owned it, but now I wasn't scared. I was furiously angry.

The kids were so upset at having to go. Devon had begun to vomit in the toilet and kept dry retching, her little arms wrapped around my legs as she clung to me. Matthew stood quietly chewing his nails, his only outward sign of distress, and Jasmine just stood there sullen. I knew she would make him pay and that thought made me afraid for her. There was nothing I could do, and he knew it. He had found the ultimate weapon. Tears ran down my cheeks as I felt so heartbreakingly angry.

The kids wrapped their little hands around each other and clung together. The older two were so brave and protected Devon.

I could see their little childhood bond – if they had each other, they were strong. They were little children. It broke my heart. If I had a gun I would have shot him in that moment.

Sometimes he would turn up, other times not. Sometimes he would be early to collect them, sometimes late. He called the shots. He would drop them off when he had enough of them or keep them longer when he wanted to. This was all part of his control to make sure I wasn't going out and partying, that I was always available.

I came to realise that there may be a small window of opportunity for me, so I decided to play a game of my own. If having the kids was in his mind a way to upset me, to control me, then I had to let him know it wasn't. Placing the thought in his mind that he could be doing me a favour whilst I went out 'partying' suddenly made sense. As he arrived to pick the children up one weekend I was all dressed up, looking like I was ready to go and have a good time. This was indeed far from the truth, but a little embellishment would surely help. I had blow-dried and fluffed my hair up, was wearing my tightest pair of jeans, a low cut top with just a hint of bra strap and even had a dash of lipstick on. As I saw my reflection in the mirror I knew what would happen. I had to hide the smugness from my face, no emotion, no clues.

'Where are you going?' he asked in a barely controlled voice as he got out the car. His hands and fingers twirled in agitation. I knew I had created a reaction.

'It's none of your business, it's my weekend without the kids,' I replied rather flippantly. I embraced an air of nonchalance as my hand reached up to flick my hair in a carefree manner.

That was all it took. He went nuts.

'You are nothing more than a slut, and if you think I am watching the kids while you slut around, then I'm not.' With that he turned and left, leaving the children standing in the driveway with their overnight bags.

The children looked at me nonplussed as I gave them a big smile and ushered them back into our home. I stripped off my pretend party clothes, the kids dumped their weekend bags and we shared a big hug and a laugh. We had won. On this day the kids and I made up our own motto, *'We always win.'* It was to be our secret catch cry many times in the years ahead.

His weekend access visits became almost non-existent. He would occasionally turn up to visit the kids, but he would only ever have them during the day and rarely for a sleepover, just in case I was 'slutting around', as he so eloquently called it.

In the summer of 1988 he then moved to Melbourne and we enjoyed relative quiet for a while, as he was engrossed with a new lady friend. But that quiet was not to last long. He just changed tactics. He decided that he had found a new mother for the children, and again started to request access and custody. He also became a frequent caller to child protection services, requesting they follow up my abuse and neglect of the children. From afar he would once again challenge for access, and a new custody battle began.

15

RUN FAT NANNY, RUN

Four years later in the early winter of 1989, I was growing weary of the need to be hyper alert and of the continual games. Lying in bed, curtains closed tight, I would hear the phone ring incessantly, the shrill sound rattling my nerves. I knew it was him.

At times if he called in the day I would innocently answer it, concerned it may be the school ringing me. Eyeing the phone with some trepidation, I would answer it to be met with a torrent of abuse and threats. Other times he would just call up to 20 times a day, then hang up if I answered. Leaving the phone off the hook to stop the feelings of anxiety building up within me, it defeated the purpose of having a phone. What if the children needed me? What if something was happening to them? How would I know? Fear and dread clogged my mind.

Eventually I ended up getting a silent number, so the phone calls then started to family and friends until they, too, had to install silent numbers. I again isolated myself from people, as I felt because of their association with me, their lives were becoming problematic. You needed a thick skin to be my friend.

He was still controlling my life in subtle ways. I couldn't understand how it could keep happening and why it was not stopped. I thought back to when I had such confidence in that stamped and sealed restraining order. I may as well have been carrying around a roll of toilet paper for all it was worth. Every other weekend there was some incident that occurred. This led to visits to my solicitor, seeking legal aid assistance followed by more court appearances. More *he said, she said*, and I was tired of it all.

Due to his erratic behaviour and threatening letters, the courts decided that pick-up and drop-off of the children would now need to take place at the Geelong police station. This also meant the onus was placed on me to travel the 36km each way into town. A year prior, I had saved up $400 to buy a blue box Cortina, my first car. Those trips into town were a constant source of stress, both financially and the guesswork of whether the car would break down or if we would even make it. The children would be really annoyed at having to go visit their dad and would play up in the car all the way in, or play their annoying games to push my already stressed-out buttons. If they weren't annoying each other, they would be highly anxious and I would have to reassure them it would be OK, that it would not be forever.

One of my main concerns was his drinking and driving with the children in the car. I felt ill at the thought of him having an accident and harming the kids. No one would take my concerns seriously. I was beginning to look like a vindictive bitch, a complaining shrew.

The courts deemed that collection of the children would take place at 11am each Saturday morning, and drop-off would be at 6pm on Sunday. On one particular Sunday whilst visiting my mother, I received a phone call in the early afternoon to say he would not be returning the children, as they were his children and he would be keeping them. He had found a better mother for them. I tried to reason with him, begging him to think of the children and follow the court orders.

Driving in panic to the police station, I begged for assistance, repeating the conversation we'd previously had regarding him not being there at six to drop the children off.

'It is only 3pm,' the officer replied. 'There's nothing we can do at the moment – he has them till 6.' The officer stood behind the counter, eyeing me with disinterest while absently fiddling with paperwork.

I tried to explain yet again that he was not going to bring the children back to me, my voice shrill and excitable. No matter how hard I tried, I just couldn't be cool or seem rational.

'Wait till 6,' he replied, then, gathering his papers, he banged them into a tidy bunch and walked away.

I returned to my mother's nearby home in a state of agitation. Despite her offers of a cup of tea to cure all ills, I continued to pace, watching the clock slowly wind down to 6pm. The big brass clock, with its pointy fingers reflecting where the numbers should be, stood out against Mum's psychedelic wallpaper. Each minute the hands of time would shudder into place, adding to my churning nerves. I could stand it no longer, and at 5:55pm I returned to the police station. It was a new officer behind the counter. I mentioned the previous visit I had made and the phone call I had received.

'I am here to collect my children,' I stated as assertively as I could, sounding more together than I felt. 'But as I have told an officer already, he has phoned me – he is keeping the children in Melbourne and stated that he will not be returning them. I have sole custody of the children and I want my children back now.' I produced the court stamped custody papers with a grand flourish, resisting the desire to smack them in the policeman's expressionless face.

The policeman gave a backwards glance toward the big clock on the wall. 'It's not quite 6pm,' was his nonchalant reply. 'He is coming from Melbourne. Be fair.'

Redness flushed my face and my hands shook as I could barely contain my anger. I sat myself on a cold bench seat and glared at the officer as he went about his business. I wasn't going anywhere.

I kept checking my watch, waiting until half an hour had passed. That was enough for me. My body was constricting and aching as it began to cramp with stress. I rose from the bench, made my way back to the counter and insisted the police ring him. The policeman retreated to make the call. I could see him watching me from behind the screen, his eye brows raised, giving a nod here and there as he watched me. I felt a sense of unease.

'I have just spoken to your husband,' he said as he returned. 'He says he explained to you that he had car trouble, but he will be here in about forty-five minutes.' The policeman's voice was calm and controlled, not a hint of concern.

I looked at him, my mouth open and closing like a dyeing goldfish, gasping for air. That's how out of my depth I felt, swimming in lies. 'He's not my husband,' was all I could manage.

'I suggest you go home and calm down. He will be here in one hour,' the policeman said.

'But the court orders say they should be here,' I ventured meekly. I knew better than to argue the point. The court orders and these papers were useless.

I again returned to my mother's home and waited. The slow ticking clock became my focus and fixation. As the minutes ticked by, I received another phone call.

'You better watch your back, bitch. I won't be there with the kids, but me and me mates will be there for you,' he snarled down the phone. 'Your time is coming, slut.'

Drained and emotionally spent, I again returned to the police station, but this time with my mother in tow. She had also had enough of this circus. I needed her moral support, and she would tell them off good and proper. I knew I spoke the truth, but no one would believe me. My mum would sort them out. The police's indifference made me feel like a liar, a drama queen, belittled and worthless. I wondered if they had a big dossier on me, a secret file marked 'troublemaker' in big black bold Texta.

As I drove to the police station, I reflected on the events of a few months prior. We had once again been in court, as I was putting in place yet another breach of the restraining order due to him constantly coming to my home in Anglesea. I had returned from hospital a few days prior and my friend Sandi B was coming to help me out, catch up for a cuppa and, as her daughter and Devon were kinder friends, they were having a play.

As we sat in the kitchen, the slow knock on the lounge room window started. Startled we looked up to see him pacing around outside the window, rattling the front door, trying to gain entry. In his hand he had a machete and started to make threats to kill me. Poor Sandi was shocked beyond belief, and I urged her to grab the children and hide at the back of the house in the laundry, ensuring the back door was locked and all the windows secure. As I was recovering from an operation my movements were slow.

Hearing the back gates slam shut, I knew he had made his way to the back kitchen window. He banged and yelled, waving the machete. I could hear the children crying as my shaking fingers dialed the police for urgent help. Sandi had locked herself and the children in the toilet, with the children cowering behind the door and Devon vomiting into the toilet in fear. She was doing a great job of protecting them from the crazy man outside. He was making his way to the back door, yelling and banging. They all started to scream. I made my way to the front windows, calling to him, trying to lure him from the back area and have his anger and threats focused on me.

Eventually the police came, but he had again disappeared. The police took our statements and poor Sandi was traumatised. It was still hard work being my friend.

This event still effects Devon thirty five years later – she can recall the date and year it happened.

When the matter came to court he stood up and, as clear and composed as could be, stated, 'Your honour, I keep going around there as she actually keeps inviting me to share the matrimonial bed. She has also given me pox from her sleeping around, so I was a bit angry.'

The slow creep of heat rose from my neck, my face reddened. I wanted to crawl in a corner or be swallowed up in a huge sink hole, be anywhere but this place. I felt the eyes of the court on me, I saw his smirk. He had achieved his intent. *Matrimonial bed? The pox? Who uses that language? Who says that?*

I was mortified, embarrassed by his untruths and he knew it. He had this ability to tell lies better than I could tell the truth. However, the judge on this occasion was not impressed by his court theatrics, and it was agreed that if he broke the restraining order again, he would face two years jail. He was not permitted to phone, harass, stalk or be within five kilometres of where I was.

Yet here I was again, waiting for him to return the children to me, an unwilling participant in his stupid game.

Parking the car down the street, Mum and I began to walk towards the police station. The whispered sound of breaking twigs made me turn in time to see him jump from behind a bush. My mind registered there was two of them. I caught a glimpse of the children with someone down the end of the street. My urge was to go to them, but fear, shock and survival set in.

I yelled to my mum, *'Run, just run. Get back to the car.'* We ran like I never knew we could, terror and adrenaline kicking in.

'Run fat nanny, run!' he yelled after us. I never stopped to look behind me. Grabbing Mum's hand, we just kept running till we made it to the car.

'Run fat nanny, run.' His words echoed in the night until the car became our sanctuary. Locking the car doors, I sped along the roads regardless of the colour of traffic lights and any other traffic. I wanted the police to pull me over, I dared them. We arrived at Mum's home, breathless and afraid. Adrenaline still coursing through my veins, I rang the police station to explain what had happened.

'But he is here waiting for you,' the officer replied. 'He has the children, he's waiting for you to collect them. You are late.'

I drove to the police station and saw three little children sitting alone on a wooden bench under the watchful eye of the policeman, clutching their little bags. I wanted to scream, swear and rage at the police, but I knew it would mean nothing, get me nowhere. Instead I held my hand out to the children and we walked silently out of that station.

Would this torment ever stop? When?

These events would continue for a few more years in varying forms of harassment and abuse, until I stood atop a gravel road and begged him to kill me, to put an end to these maddening games.

1973 – Myself and little brother Brian at my parents home. It would be a long journey home.

1996 -97 Me and the kids in the glorious years of madness.

1981 Devon and I – most of my waking moments were spent thinking of escape, I always had my baby close by.

Anglesea – to this day it remains the most beautiful sight in the world.

16

SETTLING IN – A NEW LIFE

Despite the spectre of him in the background, it was a wonderful time in many ways. For all its poverty and struggle, it was the best of times. Needing to feel settled and believe that things would be OK, I started to plan for routine and our future. Life began to swing into being. Eventually I purchased a bed for myself on layby at the second-hand shop and had managed to pay off my bargain drawers.

Winter was coming, so I needed to watch my spending. The children would need warm clothes and I needed to pay the bills. My weekly income at this time was $138.95 per week.

I had learnt many ways to cut costs with food and attempt to eat balanced, affordable meals. However, there were many times I went hungry. Mince, potatoes and pasta were our friends, and frozen vegetables, onion and rice would make an amazing amount of delicious fried rice to fill us up. As the children were growing and eating all and sundry, by the end of the fortnightly pension we would be desperate to find a good meal. The first things to go would be vegetables and meat, cheese etc. We would often also be running out of jam or Vegemite and butter. Milk and Weet-Bix would sometimes be an evening meal.

It was during this time and a week of poverty that I came up with something uniquely us. It would be forever our culinary delight – 'chewy bread.'

There is something so deliciously yummy about fresh bread straight from the bakery —warm, soft and chewy. Having run out of butter, I needed the kids to get on board with the idea, and so it came to be that 'chewy bread' was invented. I told the kids how I had gone to the local shop and found this amazing bread. It was like chewing gum, and you didn't have butter with it because that wrecked the chewiness. You just ate it by itself – nothing else was needed.

Giving them each a piece of fresh bread, I showed them how you removed the crust to eat it last, as you started by chewing on the soft inside. It was indeed delicious – just like chewing gum, only better. The kids happily chewed away, and so chewy bread was born. Even when we had butter, chewy bread was preferred. Many years later, it would become the source of some great stories, but at the time it was means to an end.

As we settled in for our first winter in our home the winds would howl along the cliffs, and to me it would always be the most beautiful time. The rains would fall in horizontal sheets and the thunder would put on quite a show. We would rug up and walk everywhere as I didn't have the luxury of owning a car in those simpler times, nor did I feel the need. Curling up like a family of contented felines by the wall heater, filling our tummies with warm stew and chewy bread, the days and evenings were so peaceful. The children could play and have friends over, and they were enjoying this new experience. I could see their confidence grow with this new freedom. They were all settled into the routines of life with school and kinder, and I was beginning to form small friendships. Paula would come over daily and we would have coffee and laughter.

Each season bought new delights, new experiences. Each new purchase of secondhand furniture became a grand occasion. No matter how rich you may become in later life, nothing will ever compare to these times of pure exhilaration at adding to our mismatched belongings.

As the first year in our home ended the seasons began to change, and winter turned into the most beautiful time of all – spring. It was during this time we discovered freesias, the sweetest smelling flower that grew wild in the bush. The kids would pick me bunches all the time, and they are a lingering memory of those days. Bunches would sit in old vases or broken cups throughout the house, their perfume evoking such comfort. I would love those beautiful spring days – the luscious smells, the sounds of nature, the crunch of gravel underfoot and the pure freedom of breathing air and seeing colour. How I loved it.

Etched in my memory is the beautiful sun as it would stream into the lounge room windows. I would lie on the floor like a contented cat, just watching and basking in that light. I made a refuge in the garden and planted trees and plants. The kids would play games or cricket in the driveway outside, building tree swings and cubbies in the bush. Their voices would carry across the heathland, yelling and laughing with freedom and abandon.

The gravel road would become hot in the sun and I would warn the kids to watch out for the occasional snake that would sun itself on the crunchy red rocks. The kangaroos would come up from the heathland to graze on the grass or to get close to the water. It was a wonderful window of life in my beautiful home and I was happy in my soul. The end of the year rolled along and soon the summer months would be here – beaches, school holidays, the New Year ahead. Jasmine and Matthew would go to school and Devon would start kinder. These were the times I cherished when it was just us – no games, no him.

This was the way it could be. This was the way forward and time rolled on.

For the first time I would have all the kids at kinder and school.
Alone, for the first time.

17

THURSDAY NIGHT

Against the backdrop of permed hair, bubblegum jeans, bulky jumpers and shoulder pads, the eighties rolled on and with it the routine of our lives. Every Thursday night, the children would be in bed, bathed and fed by 7:30. Paula would leave her children at home with her silent husband and I would wait patiently until Paula came roaring up the driveway in her husband's sporty red car. She'd come up to the house, beers in a brown paper bag tucked under her arm. From the fridge I would get my one can of rum and Coke and rustle up our weekly treat of peanuts and chips. We would both be in our pyjamas and settle in our comfy chairs, curtains drawn – we were ready. Spot on 8:30pm – so it started: the theme song from *Prisoner*.

We would smile at each other with pure glee, anticipating the drama, the shared laughter over the plot twists and the magnificent over-acting. Paula and I so loved this show – more importantly, the ritual of friendship that belonged with it. It was our time to remove ourselves from everyday humdrum.

One cold Thursday evening just as the show started, we were interrupted by thumping on the front door. In panic I thought it was him, but instead looked up to see six burly men and a woman come barging in. They flashed badges, identifying themselves as detectives.

Paula and I had jumped in fright at the initial sound, and froze in terror as they swarmed through the house. After my initial shock had subsided, I managed to enquire of their intent as they searched through kitchen drawers and emptied my handbag, its contents sprawled across the kitchen table. Apparently these detectives belonged to the drug squad, and I was being raided after an anonymous tip off that I was a drug dealer and there was a large quantity of drugs in the house that I was selling to the young locals. Was that it? Me, a drug dealer? I was on par with Pollyanna in the good behaviour stakes at this time in my life. I'd never so much had a parking ticket. I came to the obvious conclusion that it was my ex-husband playing another of his silly games.

As they searched through the house, I requested they at least be quiet as my children were in bed and I didn't want them to be upset or disturbed. The detectives searched inside cupboards, ran their hands between the couch seats as Paula and I watched trying to keep one eye on the TV. A policewoman then frisked me and followed it up with a strip search as she led me to my bedroom. After coming back clear as I knew I would, I let them know not only was this a waste of their time, but also shoddy detective work. Sitting back down on the couch, I turned my attention back to *Prisoner*. After another fruitless search and leaving behind the mess they had created, they finally left with somewhat of an apology.

The next Thursday I went through the usual motions of setting up our night, when to my amazement I saw Paula arrive in a gown split to the thigh, dripping with jewels, sequins and baubles. I looked at her, stunned.

'Just in case it's the vice squad this week,' she smiled, and we fell about laughing as we waited for *Prisoner* to begin.

18

UNDER THE KITCHEN SINK

It started as one of those usual winter colds that as a parent you just need to push through. I had no time for sickness and tried desperately to ignore it. There was too much going on in my life to take a moment and recuperate. I just had to keep going, and the stress continued to run me down.

Meanwhile, he continued to do small annoying things to disrupt my life; however I had managed to exist in a somewhat functioning manner. Forming friendships and experiencing new opportunities, I continued to embrace this busy life I had once dreamed of. The children were well settled and did not seem to have a care in the world. Access to their dad was becoming less and less, and Jasmine had gone to court to state that she would not go and see him. After several psychiatric reports and counselling sessions, it was agreed that Jasmine was capable of making her own decisions and could refuse attending his access visits. The tipping point for Jasmine was when he broke her Madonna record.

At this time his favourite way to interrupt my life was to call child protection services on me and make false claims. I became super paranoid about this as I nearly was caught out. After getting the children off to school one morning I had not had time to clean up – the beds were unmade, clothing was scattered on the floor throughout the bathroom and bedrooms, and the dishes were still on the bench and table from the night before. Happy to leave it all behind to do later, I headed off with Paula on one of our adventures. When I returned I noted the orange calling card of protective services, who had called to do a house inspection and talk to me. As I entered my home I saw it from their eyes – it was such a mess. I was so thankful I wasn't home – they would have taken the children off me for being a neglectful mother. My anxiety and paranoia about this fixated into always having a clean house. Eventually child services did call around and, as I had signed declarations from teachers, doctors and other character references on my ability to parent, they closed the file on me. Still I remained alert and neurotic.

In the winter of 1990, my cold grew worse. If only I could shake it. Anglesea, with its wonderful trees and flora, was also a great cesspit of pollens and grasses which, during this winter season, seemed to induce my long dormant asthma. The cold then found its way to my chest and I succumbed to a few day's bed rest. Sandi B and Paula took turns to help with the kids and the school runs, and I recovered soon after.

A few weeks after I had recovered from my illness, though, I started to get strong headaches. With the lounge room curtains drawn tight to block out the day, I lay on the couch trying to minimise light and sound, incapable of looking after myself or the children. *What if he came now? I couldn't save myself.* With that thought I would drift off to sleep, too tired to fight, barely remembering if I had locked the doors, too tired to care.

At one stage I awoke after seemingly being asleep for twenty-four hours to find my children had disappeared. The house was in darkness and they were gone. Immediately the choking panic invaded my lungs. Frantically I searched around the house until I came across a note scrawled in childish writing.

It informed me that they were staying at a neighbour's house and to ring when I awoke. After calling the neighbour it seemed I was not able to be woken. Concerned for the children being left to fend for themselves, and just thinking I needed a good sleep, she'd decided to leave the note and provide them with somewhere to play and a good meal.

Anglesea was a great community in this regard. A friend used to say it would be hard to steal my children. When he picked them up from school he was stopped by every second mother, wanting to know everything about him and why he had the children.

This sense of community gave me comfort.

Sandi B called around one morning to find me rolling around on the floor, clutching my head due to a smashing headache. I was also unable to see properly. I was so unwell she called an ambulance and I was taken to hospital. Sandi's barometer for knowing I was really sick was that I was even willing to leave my house messy. I had been fastidious in keeping a clean house since the child protection visits, but because I had been unwell for a few weeks I had thrown in the towel. On top of the messy house, the children's pet cat had birthed five kittens that were running rampant, so there was cat mess everywhere.

I left all the chaos behind as I closed my eyes and willingly let the ambulance take me away. After a few tests and some poking and prodding, I was sent home several hours later as apparently nothing was wrong. Sandi B came to collect me in her little car that seemed to take forever to get me home. We ended up pulling over on the side of the road several times as I vomited and rolled in agony with headaches. On arriving home, I called my doctor to come and take the pain away, knowing that I would be better cared for with my own doctor doing home visits. I put myself to bed, feeling so very ill. I thought I was dying. *Who would watch the children?* With this panicked thought, I promptly fell asleep.

It would be three and a half weeks later when I would slowly start to come out of the oblivion I had been in. As I slowly opened my eyes to the pale lilac of my bedroom, filtered light making its way through the curtain, I felt the sheets between my fingers and gripped them as I tried to get up. I couldn't move, and again closed my eyes as I fell back on the softness of my bed.

I had vague memories of voices and conversations. I remembered Paula coming to my bedside whispering, *'Don't die yet, Janabelle. You should see the shit under your kitchen sink, you need to clean it up.'* I tried to smile and answer back, but everything went to darkness again and under the kitchen sink didn't matter so much anymore. I remembered the children crying as they told me one of the kittens they had named Bullyboy had died.

Our neighbour had put the kittens outside to fend for themselves in an attempt to clean the house up. We would never have done that, the children treated them like babies. I knew the kids would have made the neighbour pay for that. I remembered Matthew telling me he had won a tennis tournament, and also not to die. I had flashes of activity and sounds around me, but I mainly slept.

I finally opened my eyes to see my mum moving around my house. I could hear her voice and was confused – she was arguing with Devon, one of their usual last word arguments that I found so pointless. They were so the same, but could not see it. Again I gingerly tried to swing my legs, hoping to be able to walk to where they were, but I could not walk. Falling backwards, I cried out in shock. My mum came into the room, her eyes so blue, lines etched on her face. She looked very tired and worried.

'You've come back to join us, have you?' she asked, and I could hear the sound of happiness and relief in her voice. As much as she tried to hold the kids back, they flew into the room to see me. I reached out for them, noticing my long scrawny fingers. They sat on the edge of the bed with their big smiling faces and chattery voices.

'Don't all crowd your mother,' Mum bristled as she busied herself around the bed. 'She needs to get well properly.'

Mum told me that I had been asleep for three and a half weeks, and as she'd been concerned for the children thought she needed to come look after us all. Mum also believed she was in training to have them full time, as at one stage she thought I was going to die. *Maybe that's what the look of relief was from,* I thought amusingly – not having to have them full time after all. I held Mum's hand, thankful that she cared for them and kept them away from him, assuming both responsibility and guardianship. Mum had also been well cared for and supported by my wonderful friends and the community, who had kept her supplied with meals, shopping and lifts to and from school. Mum also happened to mention that she had to clean my house up, which of course was a 'bloody mess.' Trust me to get caught out. I dreaded them looking under the kitchen sink, which is where I just pushed all my crap. I resisted the urge to laugh as I felt like a naughty child again, berated for having a messy bedroom.

I tentatively had to learn to find my feet and walk again with the aid of a walking stick. I could not stand the taste or smell of coffee which I had previously loved, and during my long sleep I had lost a significant amount of weight. Paula and Sandi B came to visit and spend time with me, and helped me put things in place to allow Mum to finally go home, back to her clean, quiet house. The children took great relish in telling me all the mean things that Nannie had done to them as she had invoked her 'Nannie rules'. I roared laughing at their indignation at having to be ready for bed at 6pm in their pyjamas, how and what she had packed in their lunch boxes, that she'd made them eat sprouts and spinach, and how the kittens couldn't be cuddled in their beds, among a whole list of other grievances. Nannie certainly would not have put up with their nonsense. They would surely appreciate me more.

It was a slow road to recovery and after two weeks walking with a stick I was relieved to find my feet. It took many more months to enjoy a coffee. This health scare sent me into obsessing about death – what would happen if I died, who would look after the children like I do. Even they acknowledged that they were spoilt by me, as I was the best mum ever. There was a good life lesson in all of this for the kids, and I milked it for a few weeks.

For a while I started to take my health seriously, but as stress, poverty and lifestyle take over, you just get busy with the business of living.

19

KILL ME NOW

As the summer of 1990 approached, I stood alone in the middle of the gravel road, tired of having to escape, of having to hide. I was drained from having to be alert, from the constant appearance of child protection agencies, drug squads or other agencies and departments, who seemed to have nothing better to do than check up on me and follow up on random 'tip offs'. There seemed to be no relief, no rest. The constant effort required to refute these claims, go through the court system, organise a solicitor, arrange transport, make sure I had babysitters to once again face pointless court proceedings, was taking its toll.

On top of this, yet another letter from him had arrived in the mail, warning me of my imminent demise. These rambling threats were now a weekly occurrence.

I had caught a glimpse of myself in the fading mist of the bathroom mirror that morning – I looked the way I had a long time ago, in another life. *Had it really been five years ago?* It had seemed another lifetime since I had left, but here we were again. Running, hiding, shaking with fear, hiding the children from the vulgarities of life … the dark side.

Oh, to just wake up and feel the beauty of a fresh day, laze around, walk outside freely without making sure everything was locked, that there were no entry points, I wasn't being watched or followed, jumping at sounds and shadows.

I was forever looking over my shoulder, chills up my spine, watching, waiting, seeming to be in a constant state of holding my breath, always anticipating when my time would be up. I had made a will just in case, planning life for my children after my death. I became obsessively organised.

I sighed deeply, the breath reaching deep inside my lungs. I felt beaten, emotionally spent and, in truth, probably a bit sorry for myself. How had I let this continue? How come I could not break free – was it me? The negative voices were getting into my head again as the torment continued.

It came to be on this warm Saturday morning, on what should have been a lazy summer's day, that I had received yet another message that my days was numbered, however this time it was followed by a visit from the police. He had also called the police station, warning them of something taking place at my address.

As I lounged in the calming sunshine of the lounge room floor, I was startled to see the flash of the police vehicle, followed by the stomp of police boots as they approached the verandah.

'We think you should go out of town and stay with a friend, just for a couple of hours,' the policeman spoke quite calmly. 'It's best to be safe.'

'I'm not going,' I replied and squared my chin, gritting my teeth in defiance. 'I've had enough, he can kill me. I'm tired of running. Why can't you do something to protect me for once? Five fucking years this has been going on.'

'Jan, we can't just stay here till he decides to visit.' he replied. 'What if you just call us when he arrives?' I rolled my eyes in a sullen response. 'Our recommendation is that you leave, take the kiddies and be safe.'

I stayed.

For the remainder of the day I was on high alert, the old feelings of anxiety and that awful sickness in the stomach returning. I kept the children close by. I walked around the house, checking windows were locked and the sticks of dowel I had placed in them for extra safety were wedged in tight. All doors were locked as I encouraged the children to play inside, bribing them with food and treats despite their protests to get on their bikes and visit their friends around the corner. My heart felt like it stopped at every noise. My body jumped and twitched, heart thumping against my chest, the bile of sickness burning in my stomach. *Is this living? Is this how it will always be?* I walked around my house, looking at the kids' drawings pinned against the kitchen wall. I rearranged the kitchen benches, cast an eye over the calendar for no particular reason, aimlessly looking at pieces of my life. I heard the kids playing in their rooms – maybe if I was not around, the kids would have a more settled life.

It was just after lunchtime, as the warmth of the day was closing in on the locked up house, that I heard a knock on the door. My body stiffened – was this him?

Apprehensive, I slowly moved the curtain to look out the window. To my surprise and confusion it wasn't him. Some strange man with scraggly hair, mottled beard and scruffy clothes was standing rather uncomfortably on my doorstep, a lit cigarette in his hand. He gave me a nod as he looked me in the eyes rather nervously.

'Just letting you know your husband sent me here. I'm his mate, and I'm going to take the kids for chips and hamburgers.'

I stared at him. Did he seriously think I was just going to hand my children over like that, no questions, no fight? And who the hell did he think he was, invading my home, my space?

'Fuck off,' I screamed at him, like the screaming mad woman he had no doubt heard all about. 'Just fuck off from my house.'

He looked surprised as he seemed to register this was not as simple a task as he'd been led to believe. He almost fell down the steps in his haste to get away.

The children came out from their bedrooms, their eyes wide as they'd heard me screaming obscenities. I warned them to stay inside and keep the doors locked. Their frightened faces registered briefly in my white hot rage, so I assured them it was going to be OK. For some strange reason, in my heart I knew it would be. With the full force of my anger I marched outside, swinging my arms and stomping my feet until I stood in the middle of the road. With the hot sun on my back and the comforting crunch of gravel under my feet, I knew this was the moment. I was in my space, my home, and I breathed in the sun's rays and waited.

I saw him approach me, a stalking animal circling, watching, ready to pounce. I stood still, unafraid, and spoke in a calm voice with a strength that belied my churning stomach, my racing heart.

I splayed my hands to the side, offering an open heart, a clear target, my feet planted a foot apart. 'Go on – kill me, if that is what you want, what you have threatened to do for so long. Do it, kill me, now is your chance.'

I stared him down. Steel on the outside, yet my legs were wobbling and shaking with fear. *What if he did?* The thought passed through my mind in a fleeting second, and my nerve faltered. I stilled my instinct to run, to show fear. I was tired of it all; this life of running and fear was drip-feed torture. It had to stop.

He looked at me for what seemed an age. I continued my stillness, eyes focused on him, still alert.

'Kill me then, if that's what you want. The children won't have a mother, but you won't have them either. You will be in jail. You will lose them, too, and they will hate you forever.' A defense I believed would chip away at his thoughts, distract him. By now his scruffy mate had scuttled away, the situation maybe not quite what he was anticipating. Who knows what he had been told.

I stood on that hill, the gravel under foot, surrounded by my sacred space, the warm sun on my body and I felt some inner power. I felt the shift – the moment changed.

'You're not worth jail time, you ugly mole,' was his only response, and with that he turned on his heels and walked away.

I stood there and watched as he walked down the hill. Only after I saw him disappear for good did I grip my stomach and double over in relief, my bravado finally drained from my being. *Was that it? Was it over now?*

He had the perfect opportunity to kill me and yet he let me go.

I learnt something important that day, how to finally play bluff. Once inside the safety of our home, the children all looked up at me, waiting for my lead, the cues as to what was to happen next.

'No more running away kids,' I reassured them. 'Daddy is going to stop being so silly. Let's find something to eat.'

With that, we opened the curtains, the sun shone through the windows and the day continued. The status quo had been reached for now.

20

THE SLUT OF RAMSAY STREET

In the dark confines of the local post office, with its fluorescent light flickering overhead, I stared at the envelope as it was pushed along the faded wooden bench top. Lowering my eyes, I glanced sideways to see who standing around me may have seen the letter. The look on the post mistress's face told me she had. Snatching it from the counter, I hung my head, colour rising from my cheeks. And there it was again, that unmistakable angry handwriting in extra bold black pen, jumping out from the whiteness of the envelope.

Can writing be angry? I am certain that it can – the pressure of the pen barely controlled with an inner rage and anger, the odd shaped scribble of the letters hiding a range of emotions. The hatred in the words all jumped out at me as I stared at the envelope.

To the SLUT of RAMSAY street.

As a magnet seeks out a hidden metal, such was my compulsion to open the letter. I knew the words inside would be twisted, hateful, hurtful – but I had to see, in case there was a clue. Tucking the envelope in my jeans pocket, I made my way home. The embarrassment would be mine only as I sat down, swallowed by the comfort of my chair to read the letter:

You can show this to any little idiot you like hopefully the filth cause on Friday night if you don't give me my legal rights and give me my kids you will be dealt with and if of course you won't be there your house will be burnt to the ground your mother is already getting a hiding your old man's grave will be demolished and I will never stop ever to see my children you have 4 days I don't care about any pigs or any law at all you will be beaten and you'll suffer .

That was it – short, sharp, to the point.

I had left him three years prior. Would it ever stop? I made yet another appointment to seek Legal Aid and go to court.

***

Days later, another letter arrived.

Hello Darling, I'm gonna come round and see ya soon if you like it or not I'll behave so don't worry and I don't really care if you ring the police it can't be worse than living. I'm gonna behave cause now I know how to. I love you real bad so I don't care what you think I HAVE HAD ENOUGH so I am coming to see you so you'll have to cop it.

Hello hello I don't know why you say goodbye – if you want some money I'll send it to you in 3 weeks. I have to pay for a shrink to find out why I hurt people, after I have found that out I will be ok, and hopefully we can get married again, tell Jas she has done well but I think she is a shady character and I haven't much time for her, I will move back home soon and I want to live quietly and I want to do it with you, that's if you haven't got some stooge yet but if you have I will give it a miss and get some other mole somewhere, I'd pick you first cause your sensible and fair and you don't need much, I know about the mistakes I've made but I've got it together now, if you've got a stooge boyfriend don't worry about writing back .

The absurdity of it all made me want to laugh but there was a madness to it that scared me. He knew who I had seen, where I had gone and, at times, what I had purchased, even if it was just new shoes. He wrote it all down and let me know in those never-ending letters.

Some letters would be about how he only had months to live after contracting some illness, others asking me to lend him money as he was living destitute.

In others he would try to motivate me to lead a better life, or let me know the day and time I had to stop him from committing suicide – or, alternatively, when he would kill me.

These letters would arrive sometimes daily, but generally weekly – sometimes full of undying pledges of love, others of hatred, inferred violence and ramblings of madness. Understanding the workings of a small town gossip chain, he would address the letters to cause me the utmost embarrassment – every envelope that arrived scrawled across in big bold angry pen for all to see. *The whore who has pox, the slag mother, the drug fucked slut* – the list went on, but his favourite go-to was always 'The Slut of Ramsay Street.'

He would never sign his own name, instead using creative aliases on the back of the envelope, yet leaving his address for all to see, including me.

I am sure the letters kept the poor old post mistress intrigued, and were an entertaining source of gossip within the post office walls. I could feel her eyes on me every day when I collected the mail until I eventually got a private post box, so I didn't have to go inside the post office and look at her smarmy face.

In between letters to me, he also wrote weekly to each of the children. I read them prior to handing them on, as the content was often rambling, confusing and scary. They rarely made it to the children. Instead, I would rip them into small pieces and toss them in the bin, among the kitchen scraps and other rubbish, just to ensure the kids would not be able to read them by mistake. These letters continued to arrive despite court orders stating otherwise; endless court cases with legal aid regarding breaching these orders. Not once had he been held accountable.

On 10th September 1990 (six years after leaving), I sent a letter to my solicitor asking him to withdraw all applications currently before the court. The process on my mental and physical health was wearing thin. I was tired of the game.

The letters started to dwindle away until around 1991, when a new game came into play and he decided that the children needed a new mother.

The last letter I received came from his solicitor many years later (15 years after I had left) –

22ⁿᵈ January 1999

We advise that we act for the above named who has consulted us concerning untrue and malicious statements you have been making about him in recent days.

Our client has instructed that unless we receive an apology from you in writing and an undertaking that you will not repeat such statements about him that we are to institute proceedings against you at the expiration of seven days from the date hereof.

In the event our client has instructed us to claim all his legal costs from you in relation to those proceedings. We look forward to receiving your apology and undertaking forthwith.

After receiving this letter, I felt compelled to respond:

Dear Sir,

In regard to the correspondence received 22.1.1999 I quite categorically and strenuously deny any untrue and malicious statements made about your client by myself at the alleged time in question. It is for this reason that I have no hesitation in refusing his bizarre request for an apology for an action that I am totally unaware of committing.

In the event of any legal costs incurred by your client due to his allegations, then I have no hesitation in suggesting that your financial restitution be settled by your client from fifteen years of unpaid child support and maintenance.

I await further correspondence should you wish to proceed further with this case through the legal system. If this being the case I would willingly settle this and other issues of petty harassment through the court system with all costs of undertaking these proceedings to be claimed by myself against your client.

And just like that, this game was now over. The letters had finally finished.

21

WELCOME TO THE KOALA HOTEL

For all the drama and fear that pervaded our daily lives over the years, there were also times of much joy, intense laughter and an exhilarating freedom of just living. With an almost childish glee and sense of abandon, I started to enjoy things I had never been allowed to experience, feelings and emotions that had been hidden away. As the hot sun would shine down during those languid carefree days during the season of summer 1986-87, the warmer moonlit evenings would inspire us all to embrace the crazy, the fun; and the children and I were happy to get on board an extreme ride of silliness. This was helped along in part by my younger brother Brian who, with his tribe of teenage friends, would arrive in a convoy of cars to spend their weekends at my home. What was better than a home by the beach in summer? With them they'd bring games, boxes of food and munchies, alcohol, musical instruments, and the wonderful freedom and vibrancy of youth that, in itself, becomes an addictive drug.

My brother's sole mission in life at this point was to turn my children into a form of the Von Trapp family from *The Sound of Music*. He would get his guitar, sit in the comfy chair and the children would line up before him, excited to join in the singalong. That we were several children short of his project mattered little, as they would sing, dance and laugh to the most ridiculous made up songs. My children adored him – not only was he family, but he was possibly the naughtiest adult they had ever met. The children began to appreciate the safety of family. We had never had this closeness before. Over many long weekends of playing Cluedo, Scrabble, and arguing over Charades, it is always the laughter I remember – the laughter that rips from your throat until tears roll down your cheeks and your jaw is pained with holding a smiling position. The children's eyes would just glisten with mischief.

Sometimes our fun would be interrupted by a visit from my ex, as we would be surprised by a thumping knock at the window, or a torrent of abuse would be directed at one of my brother's friends who was innocently playing ball games with the kids. The kicking of the metal side gate would give us enough notice to race inside to lock the doors. Gathering safely in the lounge room, the curtains would be drawn as we sat in a circle, and Brian would whisper made up silly songs to the children about their dad, turning it all into a secret joke or a game for the kids so it became less frightening. As his yelling and banging continued as he stalked around outside the house, we would be trying to stifle laughter, until eventually my brother had enough and would tell him to 'fuck off.' He was never that brave unless there were a few other young men around.

We were surrounded by music and noise in those carefree summer days. We had guitars leaning against the walls, a musical organ tucked in the corner and a complete drum kit placed front and centre in the lounge room. We would sing and dance like we had not a care in the world.

One of the kids' most favourite games was 'It's a Knockout', based on a TV show. My brother and whichever of his friends were visiting would set up an obstacle course throughout the house, using whatever props he could find. The house had a long passageway with all the bedrooms coming off it – the lounge and kitchen were in effect a circle that you could go around between doors. This was perfect for their game. After many hours of construction gathering blankets, washing baskets, chairs and whatever else was needed, the aim was to race their way around the course while wearing assorted items of clothing, shoes and costumes, each trying to beat the clock. This game would keep them arguing and amused for hours. On reflection it was not a very grown-up adult way of parenting, but boy it was fun. I can still see their eyes sparkling with pure glee at the joy of it all. It was a wonderful, wonderful time.

During this time, with encouragement from my brother and his friends I also started to explore the notion of going out and socialising. Sometimes they would take me to a nightclub where I just loved to dance. All this new music I heard was indeed music to my ears. I felt like I had discovered a whole new world.

One Saturday, after much encouragement from Brian, he suggested that I go to the local hotel for a catch up with some girlfriends. Brian had enthusiastically offered to babysit with another of his friends, Simon, who had joined him this particular weekend. I had a sneaking suspicion they were all up to something, as the children were also very encouraging of me to have a night out and have some fun. After ensuring they all had enough food and were settled for the night, I quickly applied a bit of makeup, threw on my dress jeans and headed out the door. Giving them all the usual do's and don'ts on the way out, I was sensing a touch of mischief as they all waved me a cheery goodbye.

Brian and the Boogers.

I had a wonderful night with my friends, just chatting about life, had a bit of a dance and after a few drinks was glad to head home. I had only just started to drink alcohol, as this was previously not 'allowed.' This was also a brave new step, the brave new me, however the shadow of him always loomed large and I always liked to stay alert, so drank minimally.

The house was in complete darkness as I arrived home. Opening the door, I nearly fell over something blocking my way. In panic, reaching along the wall I finally found the light switch, and to my surprise in front of me was Matthew's toy koala hugging a toilet roll with a sign saying, *'Welcome to the Koala Hotel.'* I tentatively went to open the lounge room door, but it would not open. I walked down the hallway passage to enter via the kitchen, and then I saw it – The Koala Hotel.

From somewhere deep inside, I heard a little voice call out, 'Mum come in, come visit us. Welcome to the Koala Hotel.'

Every single item of furniture I owned was piled in my lounge room three storeys high, into the most creative indoor cubby I have ever seen. My bed frame was holding up the second floor, the lounge suite and chairs were all turned upside down to make elaborate passageways. The kitchen table was another storey, and its chairs made more passageways with mattress walls.

'Come in Mum, come in. You have the best bedroom.'

The adult in me was really annoyed – this would take me ages to fix up. I was tired and needed to go to bed, and I certainly was not going to crawl into tiny passageways to sleep. There was clearly a mutiny happening, as the kids begged me to come join them and my brother joined in the pleas, purposely inciting them and encouraging them. I decided to crawl in, with no intention of actually sleeping there. Each child had their own room nestled within the passages and they were beyond proud of their achievements. I glared at my brother – he had the biggest grin on his face. This was just total anarchy. I made a deal – if I could just have my mattress back, they could sleep in there for one night.

The Koala Hotel has become legendary in its storytelling over the years. It was just one of the many crazy times and happy memories we had in those early years, and a welcome distraction from reality. In many ways, these times were crucial in how I learnt to live, laugh and love again.

22

LOSING IT ALL

In 1993, nine years after I had left, it seemed that my ongoing issues with him were slowly beginning to fade. The children were now older and happy to make up their own minds about whether to see him or not. Mostly they chose not to. The letters had thankfully stopped and, apart from some occasional abuse which I had heard all before, his effect on me was diminishing. I began to believe I could, in fact, have it all and do it all.

My constant need for order and control was the focus and routine of my life. It was how I coped – yet, after so many years needing to prove I was a capable mother, that I could care for my children, that I was a good person, I could cope, I was responsible – it would only be a matter of time before cracks started to appear in the facade.

The kids were now in high school, which at the time to me was a huge expense. I was working three jobs, as I wanted them to have every opportunity for a good education, and they also had increased needs, as teenagers do. I didn't want my children to miss out on life opportunities or to go without. Memories of my own experience at high school drove these thoughts, and my need for them to be 'cool' or to fit in.

During my first days of high school my father had a heart attack. In those times there was no government pension or assistance, so our family relied on the church to provide us with meals. As there was no income, our school fees were not able to be paid as required. Those students who had not paid school fees were made to sit outside the class and were not allowed to join in art, sewing or cooking. There were three of us who would sit on that bench. I burnt with anger, embarrassment and hatred at the system and the unfairness of it all. I never wanted my kids to feel that, so I worked relentlessly.

During this time I gained employment as a coordinator at the local community centre. I was very proud of this role as it gave me a new purpose, opportunities to make a difference to the community around me and, if I am honest, it provided me with a certain status and the perceived acceptance of the local community and society in general. At the time this was important to me – I had a forged a new identity. I wasn't the poor single mother with *that* ex-husband, I was just me.

I had arrived at the community centre a few years earlier – quiet, unsure of my place and raising barely a whisper. My eyes were cast downwards as I attended an information session when they had advertised the need for volunteers. The shackles that held me housebound were dragging me down, and I felt a need to belong somewhere, to put myself into society. Looking around the meeting room, the memory of the kindergarten outing flickered across my mind. Fighting what seemed my natural urge to run, I rued the fact that I had sat in the wrong chair, so escape would not be that simple. It seemed I was now stuck in the meeting, so I focused on the others who were attending, with their scarves flicked casually around there necks, all looking very much the same in a casual hippie type way. Once again, their lipsticks were smeared bright on ever talking lips, such confidence and knowing in their voices.

A shadow clouded my vision as a smiling round-faced woman stood before me, her glasses sitting at the end of her nose, the side frames tangled in her curly hair. She placed an information pack in my hands and with her warm, lemonade bubbly voice asked me what skills I had to offer.

Unprepared for the question and distracted by her giddy mannerisms, I looked into her excited face. 'I can't do much at all, I have no skills,' was my bland reply.

Of all the things to say, I had to say that, I berated myself, clutching the paperwork on my lap and purposely digging my fingertips into my jeans to distract myself with the pain. The friendly faced woman seemed unfazed, and assured me she would find me something to do. At this point, I secretly wanted her not to be so enthusiastic so I could just fly out the door; past the bright posters on the freshly painted walls showing happy, smiling people; down the ramp and continue on by the trees. If I could just keep running home to my hideaway world, life would be easier. Sitting in the back row of the meeting room, though, running away was not an option. The public mask was back in play. *I can bluff my way through this.* I smiled back and. holding the pen she offered. I signed up as a volunteer. With a flourish of grandeur, I began the first tentative steps to ease myself into a new life.

Within two years I became the coordinator – I was now the bright, smiling, welcoming face. It seems over the travels of my life, I had developed many life skills after all, in organisation and resilience. Order and control – who knew they were job skills? I was very proud of all I achieved in this role. Over the years it gave me a focus as I poured my energy and ideas into building community and developing programs that addressed areas of social justice.

As we lived in a seaside town, the community centre closed during the summer months. During this time I would wake at 5am each morning to head along to another job cleaning toilets at the local caravan park. The afternoons were then spent cleaning holiday houses. These were well paying jobs, but it was physically hard work. During the weekends I worked in a bakery – the bonus of this was that we were never without chewy bread. It seemed I was never home as I worked long and hard during those summer days, but I was able to afford nice clothes and other treats for the children. I also saved up the money to pay for their high school fees.

Having never received any financial support from him, I was their sole provider.

The children were growing into teenagers with new demands, new issues, rebellion and all the other character flaws that herald in puberty. It was becoming harder to parent in many ways. I felt that pressure building – at times it was a battlefield. My whole life seemed to revolve around providing them with what they needed and building decent humans.

Somewhere in the crazy and the need to survive, I forgot about me.

As those teenage years rolled on, I felt the crushing weight of responsibility, whether at home or at work. I became resentful of others just living what seemed to me an effortless, carefree life.

I was stuck in the moment, as people around me were going on exotic holidays, buying new cars, changing boyfriends and relationships, partying and sleeping around every weekend, buying new clothes or getting their hair done, always looking so fashionable and pretty.

Why couldn't I do that? Life seemed to be a constant struggle and grind. I still felt like the battered woman who hid in the corner at a kindergarten outing, drab and colourless. I was still living my life afraid. No matter how much I pretended or how hard I tried to fit in, I was still insignificant.

I wanted to be irresponsible, I just didn't know how.

Things began to unravel in a strange way. I missed the signs.

I heralded in the new year of 1996 feeling restless, weighted down with expectation. I made the decision to quit my job as the coordinator, I didn't want the responsibility of a community any more. Internal politics, hidden agendas, and a new wave of people into town – my internal antenna that had hid dormant started to emit signals. I didn't fit in – I was changing, and the community was changing. Retreat had become my preferred option. I craved days of isolation, long walks on the beach with my dog and not having to talk to people or think.

Within weeks of me stepping away from my job, I then experienced the ending of my friendship with Simon. We had remained close friends, in a 'relationship of sorts' as my psychiatrist would later so delightfully call it, since the time he had visited with my brother Brian all those years ago, during the days of sunshine and song. Over the last ten years Simon's friendship had been the one constant in my life, but I came to realise that this, too, was flawed. I began to question myself.

Those silent voices came back in my head, taunting me.

I believe that events of our past shape who we become, who we are. They hide somewhere in our DNA, just waiting for their chance to drag us back in to the darkness. I was fragile.

It was time for my breakdown.

I decided to embark on an irresponsible life and I embraced it with all that I had.

23

MY LOVE AFFAIR WITH MADNESS

My love affair with madness was not being helped by the scorching heat of the January sun, my newfound desire for a gin and tonic with a dash of lemon, and my new collection of assorted 'friends' who were happy to join in my 'fuck it all' theory on life.

The children were becoming concerned at this new 'Mum approach to life' where there were no rules. However, in the early days of my madness, they took full advantage of it. Jasmine wanted a caravan in the backyard – why not, let's have a teenage party house. Devon wanted penguins living in her bedroom – why not, they are cute. And Matthew played basketball at 11 o'clock at night – why not, indeed.

Who needs rules and order? I had spent the past 10 years living by them, and where had that got me?

Summer mornings were spent swimming at the beach. Hidden behind the craggy rock face I would splash in the ocean naked, arms outstretched to the blue sky, gentle sea winds caressing my face. Racing the waves back to shore, I would return to laze on the warm sand, enjoying the coolness of a gin and tonic against my parched lips, brunching on salmon and cheese platters, staring at the nothingness of a blue sky till eventually falling asleep in the hot sun. Balmy evenings would be spent singing and dancing around the fire pit, smoking dope and drinking with my newfound friends. These were all the things the sensible adult in me had warned my children against – don't go to the beach alone, don't forget sunblock, don't drink in the hot sun or you will be ill, don't drink in the daytime or you will develop a drinking problem, don't do drugs, choose your friends wisely, don't be led astray. A hundred meaningless fears had been ingrained in me to *do the right thing*. In this new life there were no rules, just the cleansing freedom of madness.

It was, in many ways, the best of the worst times – my glorious descent into madness, my escape from reality, from responsibility. How I indulged myself.

The arbor of the bush would entice me in, the smell of eucalyptus a lure forward into the hidden, uneven tracks covered by gnarly tree roots exposed from rains long ago. Sometimes I would get very lost taking the wrong trail, but by my side I would always have Evie – my beautiful dog, my best friend.

I had inherited Evie a few years prior when my older brother gifted her to Jasmine as a thirteenth birthday present. Much to my annoyance they had plotted behind my back, banking on the emotional response I would get when I saw her cute face. They were not wrong, I adored her and it was clear that Evie was indeed my dog, and I was her master. Evie was the keeper of my secrets, my comfort and friend, as well as a source of constant amusement with her silly quirks. We were a team – Evie and I against the world.

Deciding that clothes were of no particular importance to my life, I refused to get dressed, preferring instead to spend my days in pyjamas. My newfound friends would join me for day-long pyjama parties, thinking it was some great new lifestyle trend I was setting. There seemed to be no boundaries I could not push – people just joined in with the crazy. They were suffocating me with their bohemia, till the madness really took hold and the colour of life drained from my being.

At times my thoughts became so clear and I was struck with such clarity. I don't know how I descended so far down into darkness. How does it start? Maybe the human mind can only take so much – it learns how to survive on so little, it learns to think for just that one day, that one hour, that one precious minute.

My brain was running on autopilot, not allowing itself to be lost in dreaming or planning. It is the little things that send you to madness – the whispered voice, forgetting to eat, running out of milk, the sideways glance, the rustle of the trees, and the bang of a gate. The awareness, the paranoia – I was so right, I was convinced of it. The pressure had been slowly crushing me – always responsible, always doing the right thing, pay bills, work, parent, survive, never ending survival. SNAP. That was it – the colour left my world and darkness came, but with it came a delicious freedom of insanity.

I welcomed it, I embraced it. I loved it. I enjoyed the special freedom of madness as I spiraled into all its nonsense. I was going deliciously bonkers.

Who was I, what had I become? Locked away in my bush home where the sunshine once filtered through the windows, now all I saw was the dull green of the wavering gums against the backdrop of a faded wooden fence, overgrown vines creeping along the fence line, shutting out the colour and light. Curled up on a chair and shrouded in dullness, ignoring the neglected garden, I would write volumes of journals with such wisdom and clarity. At times I was stunned by my own insight and brilliance. As the shroud of darkness descended, I could feel its force looming above me, a cloud of rain before a thunderstorm sitting heavy in the sky, following me ready to release its torrent.

I knew I needed help to outrun the impending storm. After an hour of rambling to my doctor, he was concerned enough to refer me on to seek the help of a psychiatrist.

Suspicious and resentful of this turn of events, I was all set to be an unwilling participant until I met Gerald who, on having the most delightful Irish accent, would enchant and distract me continuously. Gerald would ask me strange, random questions that I was convinced had nothing to do with anything. Walking into his clinic, the comforting songs of The Cranberries would be playing in the background. This would then disarm me, oscillating between comfort and tears. Such was my fragile mind. At times I couldn't speak, the choking knot in my throat rendering me mute. I remembered that feeling from another life long ago. Across his desk with the beautiful wood grain patterns, I would push my rambling journals for him to read. As fidgety hands played with the swirling grain patterns, I would watch his face for clues, yet he would not blink an eye at the knife marks I had put through them. Gerald allowed me to indulge my misery, all the while talking to me, listening to me. His lilting accent soothed me, and his quiet presence made sense in a chaotic world. Gerald was just what I needed to set me on the road to recovery to find colour.

I thought I had all the answers during this wonderful madness, but as the mad season ended winter would come and, with it, change.

24

THE LEAVING

PART 3

It is a rare occurrence that I make a decision with my head above my heart. It is also unwise to make a life-changing decision when your head is not a well place to be. Once again, I found myself making what I believed to be grown-up decisions. With the wisdom of a new age guru, I decided to let life control my destiny. It was time to let go of my past, change my behaviours and let go of my fear.

At this time my children were now living in the city. After recovering from my lost years and having to join a functioning society, I had returned to the workforce with a job out of town. This allowed me anonymity and a chance to reinvent myself.

Travelling the 80kms to and from work five days a week opened up new challenges, as it came to be that I spent less time doing the things I loved, as life changed into another phase; working to live. Long walks in the bush and carefree days walking the beach tracks were long gone. Days of sunshine and song seemed far between, and having lost Evie in a traumatic accident my remaining weekends were now mostly spent in the city as I helped my children with various challenges that life had thrown at them.

In the cold of winter 2002, I found myself without a car and without the finances to purchase one. As there was only one bus in and out of town, or having to rely on other people for a lift to work, this became a problem to me. I am not a fan of being reliant on others, preferring to take responsibility for myself.

I was growing tired of coming home to the quiet of an empty house on cold winter nights. It seemed to highlight my loneliness and loss.

I stood small on the well-worn carpet, the sink clear from dishes, no messy fingerprints on the walls or toys laying around ready to trip me up. Glancing at the heater as I turned it on to ease the chill, I had no-one to fight for the best spot. Opening the fridge to find something to eat, I pondered why I needed such a big fridge – a half opened pack of cheese, dead tomato, collection of condiments I never seemed to use these days and a half full carton of milk barely seemed worth the effort. Shutting the fridge I grabbed some chewy bread and sat munching it on the sofa. The maroon and gold swirly couch was long gone, and the house was full of years of accumulated treasures, things I loved.

This house in Anglesea had so many memories attached to it – every room, every corner had a memory of noise, children and activity, love, loss, tears and laughter, pain and triumph. Everything I had become was etched in those walls. But now I was alone, and as the key turned in the lock each night and my hand ran along the hallway feeling for the light switch in the dark, it felt like an empty shell. There was no noise to greet me. There was silence.

I made an adult decision. I would leave the security of government housing and my safe home. After eighteen years it was time to be brave and go to live in the big world, take risks. I would move to the city. I had a good job that could afford me a private rental.

On the spur of the moment, overwhelmed with a deep sadness and nostalgia, I handed in my letter of notice. I had done it.

Scouring the newspaper rental section, I was lucky to find myself a cute little old-style cottage close to my family and close to work. The rent was rather high, but I could walk to work. I didn't need a car, so financially I could cope. I would just need to be frugal – I had done that before; that was nothing new to me.

I began to pack away parts of my life to take to a new house. I had to let some material things go as I would not need them in my new life – the children's bedroom furniture, some old wardrobes. The shed was full of junk and memorabilia, the children's school art, Jasmine's collection of relics from her teenage years, Matthew's collection of basketball and sporting magazines and cards, Devon's old toys and craft treasures – and in the corner, nestled above the makeshift shelf, was the old suitcase. Dusting off cobwebs, I marveled at its smallness. Tears stung from the corner of my eyes as an immense sadness flooded over my body, the weight causing me to falter as I separated items into piles to keep or rubbish, remnants of a life no longer lived. My memories would live in my heart – they would always be with me in the feel of the wind, the smell of the bush, the sound of crashing waves, the words of a song, the laughter of children and the screaming voices of joy and play across the heathland.

As the last week in Anglesea drew close, the pain of loss crippled my body and I started to question my decision, my stupidity. I walked along the cliff tops, the wind whipping my senses to life. The sunlight streamed through the window on a winter's day, flickering between swaying gumtrees and creating dancing shadows on the wall. I cried. I looked at my garden – the years I had toiled over creating rock spaces, garden beds, watching the trees grow from young saplings to now stand tall. It was a fortress wall around my home, just as I had once pictured back when the home was nothing but an empty shell. Tears of sorrow ran down my face. What was making me move? Arriving home to the silent coldness, in the late of night, to an empty house – despite my despair, my rational unemotional brain told me I was doing the right thing.

As I began to prepare for the big move, I packed away all the furniture and treasures I would need to make a home in my new place. I went into the garden and dug up all the garden sleepers and a big rusty tractor wheel to take with me. I just couldn't let them go or leave them behind … they had a story, a beloved memory, and I needed to cling onto them.

I had a small gathering of friends around me as I said goodbye to 18 years of my heart. As the last helpers arrived to load up their utes and trucks, I stepped away to the rest my head against the old gum on the property's boundary line, next to the crunchy gravel of the road. Closing my eyes in a moment of solitude … like a movie reel imprinted on my mind, I remembered the very first day I set eyes on this house, half built atop a hill. My heart faltered at the memory, still able to evoke such pain and sadness. I remembered the day I left it, carrying nothing but a battered old suitcase. It seemed such a long time ago, and at the time I did not know if I would ever return.

So here I was again, this time leaving by my own choice. I had made a grown-up decision ... it was time to stand up strong, live my life. The key turned in the lock for the last time as I closed the door, then walked away and sobbed. No looking back.

I settled into my new rental house in the June of 2002. In some strange twist of fate I soon learnt that he lived two streets away. I felt uneasy, unsettled.

In August of that same year I was called into a meeting at work to be informed they were closing the division of the community service that I managed, and I would be made redundant in December.

What had I done, how could I afford the rent? Why did I take a risk, why was I so stupid? Why did I not just wait two months, why didn't they tell me sooner? All these thoughts ricocheted through my mind. I was shattered. I had given up my security, my safe house. It seemed that I had come the full circle – for what?

The last few months at work became very stressful, and many staff left. I didn't have the luxury to do so as I needed the money for rent. I was stuck there. New management swept through the service and the behaviour of a certain manager was one of bullying, intimidation and overt exclusion. I became completely depleted physically and mentally, and at times a familiar feeling, long dormant, began to bubble to the surface. These triggers would always set me back. I couldn't escape them.

All my hope for a new life, a new start, was gone. I had lost everything. The misery cloud was hovering above me, following me. I could feel the darkness return. I was in trouble, I knew the signs. I had to see Gerald. I couldn't go through this again. I was breaking down.

In the January of 2003 I packed a suitcase.

I was again homeless, only now there was just me. I had put everything I had left of value in storage in a friend's garage, I packed a suitcase and moved in with my mother.

I had left that house 29 years earlier on the day I was married.

It seemed like I had made a long journey home; my suitcase and I.

I was so weary. I just needed sleep.

25

HOW TO BUILD A LIFE

I moved back into Mum's house, back into my old bedroom that I had left as a willful brat of a teenager three decades ago. The room seemed so much smaller now. There were no pop star pictures on the wall, the swirly multi-coloured wallpaper was long gone, but the brass clock with the pointy hands still stood like a beacon of longevity on the wall above the kitchen.

Like the house I had left behind in Anglesea, Mum's house was strangely quiet, but this time round it was me who added the noise to it. My brothers and sisters were long gone, and Mum spent her days at Bingo or at my sister's house – the good sister, the one who always listened and took Mum's advice.

No doubt I was again the subject of stories, a new soap opera, but these days I didn't care so much. I again seemed to be spending my days like a sullen teenager, headphones on so I didn't have to engage in conversations, listening to Eminem. During this time his music spoke to me – his angst, his fight, and his delicious obscenities against the world. It drove my Mum mad and she despaired of me not acting my age.

I purchased a secondhand shiny red push bike and spent my time wheeling around riding nowhere in particular, just anywhere to get away from the suffocating smallness of the room. My feet would furiously pedal along as I rode as fast as I could. The wind would whip in my face like the cliff walks of another life, as I went scooting through puddles, lifting my feet wide to not get wet, laughing at my efforts to avoid potholes. I would just ride with the most wonderful sense of freedom. I had forgotten how good it was to ride a bike and how childish I felt.

I was regressing, my mother was convinced of it. I continued to see Gerald weekly and ramble away my manic thoughts.

Eventually I knew, as I always seemed to know, that I had to get back to good. With the words of Eminem motivating me, I knew I had *'one shot, one opportunity. Was I gonna let it slip?'*

I again applied for public housing, as this was the only way I could see myself being able to afford to live on my own terms. I had given up my beloved home in Anglesea only six months earlier and had been an excellent tenant. Gerald wrote me a supporting letter as to why I needed to be rehoused as a priority due to my dwindling mental health – the waiting list for public housing can be up to five years and the thought of waiting that long sent me into despair. My opportunity was about to present itself. Within two months I received a letter – there was a public housing unit waiting for me if I was interested.

I peddled as fast as I could on my bike to see the unit they were offering, praying to the universe it was not in the 'druggie flats.' It was a stand-alone unit with two bedrooms and a garden. It was in ordinary condition, but I needed a challenge. I knew I could make it mine. I would have security. I would again have a home. I made my way into town to sign the paperwork and they mentioned how beautifully I had left the Anglesea house, so they knew I would be a good tenant. For once my mother's wise words echoed pleasantly in my ears – *'you reap what you sow.'* Here was my reward. I moved into the unit in May 2003 with my few remaining possessions.

Sitting on the floor of my new unit with its ugly green walls, I gazed at the sunshine streaming through the window, highlighting the stains on the faded carpet.

Alone I lovingly unpacked all the items that had been in storage for the five long months I had stayed at my mother's. It was like a Christmas morning, reacquainting myself with all the things I loved. From the tightly wrapped newspaper I gently unpacked my beautiful English tea cup trios and my coloured glass pieces that I had collected on those lazy winter weekends scouring the op shops with Simon.

I held them to my chest and gently kissed each of them – my treasures … my memories. Once again, I unpacked the three cups with the children's names on them and the ceramic china man that had stayed the course of my life travels. I still had the $36 set of drawers I had purchased when I first set up home all those years ago. I also had my garden sleepers and the big farm wheel from my Anglesea house. I placed them around the unit, making it a home.

I began once again to build my life.

The three mugs and statue I packed into the suitcase. They remain the only things I have from that life.

26

LET IT BE 2015

It was one of those bleak October days; the drizzling rain was a constant, affecting my mood and motivation. I needed to get to the shops to purchase something for dinner; such a tedious chore.

Where's Spring? I pondered, as I made a dash to my car, the rain dripping lightly on my head.

I set myself into the car to make the short trip as the windscreen wipers creaked into action. It was a short 10-minute drive to the main supermarket. I really do detest shopping and the effort involved. I was mentally going through the things I would need whilst keeping an eye on the weather conditions on the road.

I passed a couple of children riding their bikes through puddles, doing wheelies and making a great splash. I fondly remembered the times when a bike was my mode of transport and wished I could be doing the same thing. Mine now sat out in the garage. Why did I stop? Did life get busy? Did I grow up?

I saw others walking against the elements, heads down, rugged up, hurrying to where they needed to be in this miserable weather.

Ahead in the rain I saw a familiar gait – only now it was not strong, purposeful or angry, but tired and huddled with age, shuffling along, head bowed into the wind and oncoming rain. The walk of the invisible … I remember that walk. He looked so cold, wet and miserable. *I know that gait, I know that walk, and I know that person.*

I slowly pulled into the curb and rolled down the window.

'Would you like a lift, Steve? It's horrible weather.'

He turned his head, surprised.

'Thanks Jan,' he smiled, his teeth now yellowed and a few were missing. Lowering his gaze, he climbed into my car. As the seat belt was flung across his shoulder, he stopped to look at me.

'How have you been keeping?' he asked. 'You look well?'

I was surprised by how small he seemed, how frail and old. I smiled back at him as I thought of my answer, no mask needed.

'Life is good,' I replied, and I knew it was.

***

My children and I remained a fortress – unbreakable. I was surrounded by the love and joy of my grandchildren. The things that I once dreamt for in that other life – friendship, belonging, the safety and stability of home, the choice and freedom to just be – I had them all.

Time passes by. We reap what we sow, and life goes on.

No matter what we endure throughout our life – the laughter, tears, the joy and the pain – it is the threads of family and friendship that hold us together; this, and the enduring belief and hope that days of sunshine and song lie ahead.

My children – always together. We are a fortress.

EPILOGUE

I still live in the little unit where I finally set up my home, although I yearn to return to Anglesea with an ache that is hard to describe. My life is comfortable, simple and mostly joyful. My children have all now grown and I am a grandparent to eleven. We all live within fifteen minutes of each other and remain very close.

I'd like to be able to say we all went on to live a life free from the effects of what we called 'that other life,' but that would not be true. Living with family violence has an effect that stays within your DNA and shapes many experiences in later life.

I have spent a majority of my working life assisting women after fleeing domestic violence in the provision of material aid assistance to set up their homes, a service that was unheard of in my time.

I'd like to say we have progressed in supporting women and children of family violence, but again that is not true. Currently in Australia, on average one woman a week is murdered by her current or former partner. The time of highest risk is when they are leaving and 40% of women continue to experience ongoing violence even after separation. Intimate partner violence is a leading contributor to illness, disability and premature death for women aged 18 – 44. (Statistics from White Ribbon Australia)

Emergency housing is still highly under resourced, leaving many women and children at risk of homelessness.

So, when you next hear a conversation where someone says, 'She should just leave,' stop for a moment, and instead ask, 'how, as a community, can we help?'

If you are feeling unsafe or are concerned for someone's safety call

000

For confidential crisis support, information and accommodation please call safe steps 24/7 family violence response line

1800015188

For confidential phone help and referral in Australia please call

1800 7377328 (1800 RESPECT)

Call the domestic violence helpline to escape violence

1800 811 811

ACKNOWLEDGEMENTS

There are several people who have been important to me in the process of completing this book. This is my moment to acknowledge them, and to thank them for their space in bringing my story into being.

Firstly Joanne Fedler, accomplished author – who first said the immortal words to me that sparked the idea. *'You have a story to tell, you must tell it.'* Thank you for giving me the safe space, understanding and confidence to tell my story without judgement.

To my fellow Fiji writing ladies – that time was inspiring and special. I have often felt your gentle hands in the small of my back, guiding me forward.

A big heartfelt thank you to Kate, Jen and the pups, Flash, Winky and Pele for finding me a way to come home to my beloved Anglesea, where I could take time out to write the book and heal in more ways than you will ever know.

And finally, my forever tribe – Paula, Bonnie, Annemarie, Sandi B, Tom and Dee, for all the late-night conversations, inspired ideas, excellent adventures, laughter and tears. Your unconditional friendship has kept me sane over the years.

It would be remiss of me not to save my biggest thanks to my brother Brian, for always encouraging me, believing in me and hassling me to get my story told without fear or favour.

And my children. It was your story, too.

About the Author

Jan Daniels was born in the late 1950s in England, but has called Australia home for over five decades.

Jan has a deep love for the natural beauty of the country, especially of her spiritual homeland and muse, Anglesea. Raising her three children in the Surf Coast township as a sole parent gave her a solid foundation to rebuild her life and find the peace and stability she so craved.

Jan is fascinated by people, conversations, the human spirit, the seasons of life, artistic talent and reality TV. Her greatest joy comes from beauty and colour, family and belonging, the lure of clifftops and an angry sea, the will to win and her beloved Hawthorn Football Club – the longest relationship and love affair of her life.

Jan has long worked in community organisations and is currently business manager of several social enterprises.

www.ingramcontent.com/pod-product-compliance
Lightning Source LLC
Chambersburg PA
CBHW071734080526
44588CB00013B/2022